Child Abuse

Other Books in the Current Controversies Series:

Child Abuse

Bryan J. Grapes, *Book Editor*

Bonnie Szumski, *Editorial Director*
Scott Barbour, *Managing Editor*

CURRENT CONTROVERSIES

Cover photo: © FPG International

Library of Congress Cataloging-in-Publication Data

Child abuse / Bryan J. Grapes, book editor.
     p. cm. — (Current controversies)
   Includes bibliographical references and index.
   ISBN 0-7377-0678-3 (pbk. : alk. paper) — ISBN 0-7377-0679-1
(lib. bdg.)
   1. Child abuse—United States. 2. Child welfare—United States.
I. Grapes, Bryan J. II. Series.

HV6626.52 .C543   2001
362.76'0973—dc21
                                               2001023407
                                                    CIP

Contents

endangering children by making the child abuse problem appear too large to solve.

Chapter 2: What Causes Child Abuse?

Chapter 3: How Can Society Respond to Child Abuse?

substance-abuse counselors. The lifting of the confidentiality laws and adequate funding would allow child welfare officials to provide substance-abuse treatment to parents who need it.

Chapter 4: Will Changes in the Criminal Justice System Help Prevent Child Sexual Abuse?

Yes: Changes in the Criminal Justice System Will Help Prevent Child Sexual Abuse

No: Changes in the Criminal Justice System Will Not Help Prevent Child Sexual Abuse

Foreword

By definition, controversies are "discussions of questions in which opposing opinions clash" (Webster's Twentieth Century Dictionary Unabridged). Few would deny that controversies are a pervasive part of the human condition and exist on virtually every level of human enterprise. Controversies transpire between individuals and among groups, within nations and between nations. Controversies supply the grist necessary for progress by providing challenges and challengers to the status quo. They also create atmospheres where strife and warfare can flourish. A world without controversies would be a peaceful world; but it also would be, by and large, static and prosaic.

The Series' Purpose

The purpose of the Current Controversies series is to explore many of the social, political, and economic controversies dominating the national and international scenes today. Titles selected for inclusion in the series are highly focused and specific. For example, from the larger category of criminal justice, Current Controversies deals with specific topics such as police brutality, gun control, white collar crime, and others. The debates in Current Controversies also are presented in a useful, timeless fashion. Articles and book excerpts included in each title are selected if they contribute valuable, long-range ideas to the overall debate. And wherever possible, current information is enhanced with historical documents and other relevant materials. Thus, while individual titles are current in focus, every effort is made to ensure that they will not become quickly outdated. Books in the Current Controversies series will remain important resources for librarians, teachers, and students for many years.

In addition to keeping the titles focused and specific, great care is taken in the editorial format of each book in the series. Book introductions and chapter prefaces are offered to provide background material for readers. Chapters are organized around several key questions that are answered with diverse opinions representing all points on the political spectrum. Materials in each chapter include opinions in which authors clearly disagree as well as alternative opinions in which authors may agree on a broader issue but disagree on the possible solutions. In this way, the content of each volume in Current Controversies mirrors the mosaic of opinions encountered in society. Readers will quickly realize that there are many viable answers to these complex issues. By questioning each author's conclusions, students and casual readers can begin to develop the critical thinking skills so important to evaluating opinionated material.

Current Controversies is also ideal for controlled research. Each anthology in the series is composed of primary sources taken from a wide gamut of informational categories including periodicals, newspapers, books, United States and foreign government documents, and the publications of private and public organizations. Readers will find factual support for reports, debates, and research papers covering all areas of important issues. In addition, an annotated table of contents, an index, a book and periodical bibliography, and a list of organizations to contact are included in each book to expedite further research.

Perhaps more than ever before in history, people are confronted with diverse and contradictory information. During the Persian Gulf War, for example, the public was not only treated to minute-to-minute coverage of the war, it was also inundated with critiques of the coverage and countless analyses of the factors motivating U.S. involvement. Being able to sort through the plethora of opinions accompanying today's major issues, and to draw one's own conclusions, can be a complicated and frustrating struggle. It is the editors' hope that Current Controversies will help readers with this struggle.

Greenhaven Press anthologies primarily consist of previously published material taken from a variety of sources, including periodicals, books, scholarly journals, newspapers, government documents, and position papers from private and public organizations. These original sources are often edited for length and to ensure their accessibility for a young adult audience. The anthology editors also change the original titles of these works in order to clearly present the main thesis of each viewpoint and to explicitly indicate the opinion presented in the viewpoint. These alterations are made in consideration of both the reading and comprehension levels of a young adult audience. Every effort is made to ensure that Greenhaven Press accurately reflects the original intent of the authors included in this anthology.

"While some children die of neglect and abuse, most victims survive with psychic scars that stay with them throughout their lives."

Introduction

In November 2000, a San Jose man was riding in a female coworker's car when he thought he heard a child moaning. According to Sergeant Steve Dixon of the San Jose Police Department, the man "looked in the back seat. There was no one there. He looked at her [his coworker]. She looked very nervous. She began talking very loudly. He heard the moaning several times. She turned up the radio, apparently to drown out the sounds." The man later called the police, and the woman was arrested on suspicion of child endangerment after her two sons, ages five and seven, told authorities that their mother would sometimes lock them in the trunk of her Honda Civic when she went to work. In describing this incident, Dixon stated, "It's almost unbelievable."

Indeed, what is perhaps most shocking about this story is that it is only "almost" unbelievable. Due to the frequency with which one hears of child abuse cases—even cases much more serious than children being locked in the trunk of a car—the incident is frighteningly *believable*.

Statistics suggest that child abuse is not a rare occurrence. According to the National Clearinghouse on Child Abuse and Neglect Information, a resource office of the U.S. Department of Health and Human Services, there were 2,806,000 reports of possible child maltreatment in 1998. About one-third of these (34 percent) were "screened out," and about two-thirds (66 percent) were investigated. Of those investigated, about 540,000 (29.9 percent) resulted in a finding of "either substantiated or indicated child maltreatment."

The clearinghouse estimates that in 1998 903,000 children were victims of maltreatment, defined as "children who are found to have experienced or be at risk of experiencing substantiated or indicated maltreatment." This number includes 1,100 children who died of abuse and neglect. Of these 903,000 victims, over one-half (54 percent) experienced neglect, about one-fourth (23 percent) suffered physical abuse, and 12 percent were victims of sexual abuse. The remaining 11 percent were subjected to psychological abuse and medical neglect in roughly equal numbers. The vast majority (87 percent) were maltreated by one or both parents.

Advocates for abused children point to these and other statistics to support their argument that child abuse is a serious problem in America—although some insist that the problem is much more widespread than these numbers suggest. For example, Jim Hopper, a research associate at Boston University

School of Medicine, asserts that the majority of child abuse victims are not counted in official statistics because "most abused and neglected children never come to the attention of authorities." Hopper claims that sexual abuse is especially unlikely to be reported to authorities because "there may be no physical signs of harm, there is always intense shame, and secrecy is often maintained, even by adults who know of the abuse, for fear of destroying a family." For these reasons, Hopper concludes, "the statistics on 'substantiated' cases of child abuse and neglect collected by the U.S. Department of Health and Human Services are *not* indicative of actual rates of child abuse in the United States."

Others argue that the numbers actually create the impression that the problem is more severe than it actually is. Child abuse activists often cite the fact that there are about 2.8 million child abuse reports each year—an increase of about 41 percent since 1988. However, as previously stated, more than half of such reports are either screened out or found to be unsubstantiated. Moreover, the large increase since the late 1980s is largely the result of new laws that require certain professionals—such as social workers and teachers—to report every suspected case of child abuse. Since these professionals are shielded from litigation for making unsubstantiated reports, while at the same time face severe punishment if they fail to report substantiated abuse, they have an incentive to report even the most questionable cases. Douglas J. Besharov and Jacob W. Dembosky, writing in *Slate* magazine, attribute the increase in reports to a "growing reportorial sensitivity of professionals." They suggest that "professionals who become more sensitive to possible abuse, or more adept at noticing it, would make more reports . . . even if the actual incidence had not risen."

While experts debate the accuracy of the statistics, few dispute the harm that child abuse can cause. While some children die of neglect and abuse, most victims survive with psychic scars that stay with them throughout their lives. As stated by the National Council on Child Abuse and Family Violence, "Abuse robs children of the opportunity to develop healthy, trusting relationships with adults, contributes to low self-esteem, and impairs healthy psycho-social development. Indeed, the effects of childhood abuse often last a lifetime." A problem with such potentially devastating consequences deserves thoughtful scrutiny. To that end, the authors of *Child Abuse: Current Controversies* take a close look at many of the contentious debates that surround this issue, including the severity of the problem, its causes, and how best to prevent it. Throughout these pages, contributors grapple with the challenge of protecting society's most vulnerable members.

Chapter 1

Is Child Abuse a Serious Problem?

Chapter Preface

In October 2000, a seventeen-year-old boy called 911 and reported that he and his twelve-year-old brother were chained in their bedroom. When authorities arrived at their home, located in a rural desert community in California, they found that the two boys were not in chains. However, dog chains were found attached to their bedposts, and the boys had marks on their wrists suggesting they had recently been restrained. In addition, they were filthy, underdeveloped mentally and physically, and had scars on their backs.

While everyone agrees that the abuse of children in this manner is a horrible crime, many commentators disagree on how common such cases are. The National Clearinghouse on Child Abuse and Neglect Information reports that in 1998, there were 2,806,000 reports of child abuse and neglect in America. While many of these were "screened out" or found to be "unsubstantiated," the NCCANI concludes that 903,000 children were victims of maltreatment. Some argue that even these numbers do not adequately convey the extent of the problem, as many cases of abuse go unreported. For example, the sexual abuse of boys is believed to be vastly underreported. As William Holmes of the University of Pennsylvania School of Medicine explains, "Abuse of boys has not been well documented, in part because boys fear they won't be believed or will be labeled homosexual."

Others insist that child abuse advocates exaggerate the extent of the problem. Attempting to put the statistics on child abuse in perspective, K.L. Billingsley, a fellow at the Center for the Study of Popular Culture, states, "Between 95 and 99 out of every 100 children . . . are not beaten up by their parents. And more than 97 percent of all children are not abused or neglected in any way."

While all agree that the abuse of a child is a serious problem, debate continues as to the extent of child abuse in America. This issue is the topic of the following chapter.

The Incidence of Child Abuse Is Increasing

by Prevent Child Abuse America

About the author: *Prevent Child Abuse America is an association dedicated to the prevention and treatment of child abuse.*

In 1997, an estimated 3,195,000 children were reported to child protective services (CPS) agencies as alleged victims of child maltreatment. This figure is based on information collected from 35 states which indicated that each state averaged a 1.7% increase in reports between 1996 and 1997. Nationwide, the rate of children reported for child abuse or neglect increased 4% during this period, from 45 per 1,000 children in 1992 to 47 per 1,000 in 1997. Overall, the total number of reports nationwide has increased 41% since 1988.

The national increase in children reported between 1996 and 1997 is somewhat higher than the increase observed between 1995 and 1996. Overall, 17 states reported increases in the number of reports received last year, down from 18 states which reported increases in the 1996 survey. Of these 17 states, six experienced increases of 10% or more. Among them, Arizona had a 35% increase which, according to its state liaison, was primarily due to a new centralized reporting system utilizing a single hotline. Delaware's state liaison speculated that the 27% increase in reports observed in their state is likely due to a highly publicized child abuse related death that occurred in January 1997 [in November 1996, teenagers Amy Grossberg and Brian Peterson killed their newborn in a Delaware motel room]. In contrast, sixteen respondents noted actual or expected declines in their reports. Two states, Alaska and Rhode Island, reported virtually no change.

Since 1992, only two states, Delaware and Oklahoma, have experienced consistent annual increases while none of the states have experienced consistent declines. These patterns underscore the variability in reporting statistics over time and the sensitivity of this system to changes in social, political and administrative conditions or procedures.

Fifteen out of every 1,000 U.S. children were substantiated as victims of child

Excerpted from Prevent Child Abuse America, "Current Trends in Child Abuse Reporting and Fatalities: The Results of the 1997 Annual Fifty State Survey," available at www.preventchildabuse.org/50data97. html. Reprinted with permission from Prevent Child Abuse America.

maltreatment in 1997, similar to the rate reported in the prior three years. The 1997 rate is based on data from 35 states averaging a 33% substantiation rate. States which could not provide a substantiation rate for any of these years include California, Maine, Nevada, North Dakota and West Virginia. In 1997, substantiation rates ranged from a low of 10% in Kansas to a high of 56% in Kentucky. Using the 33% average substantiation rate, an estimated 1,054,000 children were substantiated as victims of child abuse and neglect in 1997, a 5% increase over the number accepted to CPS caseloads in 1996.

Factors Accounting for Reporting Changes

To help determine whether changes in reporting rates represent an actual increase/decrease in child abuse or merely reflect a more accurate assessment of the problem, we asked each liaison to name the two most significant factors which accounted for the reporting trends in their state. While these answers are not based on quantitative data, they give a descriptive appraisal of those factors CPS administrators consider the most relevant.

All of the 17 states with an increase responded to this question. Nine (or 53%) of the responding states attributed the rise in reports to increased public awareness through media and education of the reporting system which made the public as well as the mandated reporters more aware of their responsibility to report suspected child maltreatment. Reporting system

> *"An estimated 1,054,000 children were substantiated as victims of child abuse and neglect in 1997, a 5% increase over the number . . . in 1996."*

changes such as centralized intake, more effective intake assessments, the use of standardized screening tools, and newly implemented data systems represented the next most common response, cited by five (or 29%) of the responding states. In addition, four states also cited substance abuse as a major contributor to growth in reports. . . .

Breakdown by Type of Abuse

To provide appropriate prevention and treatment services, it is necessary to determine the prevalence of different types of maltreatment as well as other characteristics of the CPS caseload. Each state liaison was asked to provide a breakdown of all reported and substantiated cases by type of maltreatment for 1996 and 1997. Five categories were provided: physical abuse, sexual abuse, neglect, emotional maltreatment and other. Twenty-one states provided reporting data for both years while 30 states gave a breakdown for substantiated cases for both years. Although most of the states were able to provide data using the above-mentioned categories, a few states did not distinguish emotional maltreatment from neglect while three states included sexual abuse in the category of physical abuse.

Neglect represents the most common type of reported and substantiated form of maltreatment. In 1997, 22 states provided the following breakdown for reported cases: 52% involved neglect, 26% physical abuse, 7% sexual abuse, 4% emotional maltreatment and 11% other. For substantiated cases, 31 states gave the following breakdowns: 54% neglect, 22% physical abuse, 8% sexual abuse, 4% emotional maltreatment and 12% other. Compared to the reported cases, the substantiated cases contain a slightly higher percentage of neglect and a slightly lower percentage of physical abuse cases. Similar to the pattern observed in the past three years, these two distributions are almost identical. However, it is noted that "other" has become a bigger category in 1997 for both reported and substantiated cases than in previous years. This reflects that states are using more detailed systems in classifying types of child maltreatment. For example, behaviors included under the "other" category are abandonment, multiple types of maltreatment, imminent risk, medical and educational neglect, substance and alcohol abuse, dependency, threat of harm, and lack of supervision or bizarre discipline. . . .

> *"Neglect represents the most common type of reported and substantiated form of maltreatment."*

Primary Presenting Problems

Families reported for child maltreatment often display a number of problems which can contribute to their likelihood for engaging in abusive behavior. Identifying these problems is a first step toward prevention. To assess whether specific patterns are shared by families on CPS caseloads across the country, respondents were asked to describe the major problems presented by their caseloads. Forty-one state liaisons responded to this question with 88% (36 states) naming substance abuse as one of the top two problems exhibited by families reported for maltreatment. This percentage is higher than those reported in previous years, 76% in 1996, 81% in 1995, and 76% in 1994, suggesting that after several years of some improvement, substance abuse is again surfacing as a primary contributor to child maltreatment.

The second most frequently cited problem area noted by the respondents involved poverty and economical strains. Twenty-one liaisons (51%) indicated that their clients lack financial and transportation resources, face problems of inadequate housing and unemployment, and often have limited community resources and support. Sixteen liaisons (39%) also reported that issues of parental capacity and skills were common problems experienced by families involved in child maltreatment. More specifically, the parents in these families often lack specific parenting skills due either to various mental health problems, poor understanding of a child's normal developmental path or young maternal age. Finally, eleven liaisons (27%) reported that a significant percentage

of their adult clients struggle with domestic violence and often p\
own history of battering. . . .

Child Maltreatment Fatalities

One of the greatest tragedies is the death of a child from abuse or negle ̲ ᴀl-
though such deaths are relatively infrequent, the rate of child maltreatment fatalities confirmed by CPS agencies has risen steadily over the past eleven years.

Only 29 states were able to provide fatality data for 1997. Since data from these
states comprises less than half of the U.S. population under eighteen years of age,
we are unable to project a national fatality statistics for 1997. Based on the
twenty-five states which reported fatalities for both 1996 and 1997, there is an 8%
decrease in child maltreatment related fatalities (from 572 in 1996 to 527 in
1997). Of these 25 states, fifteen observed decline during this period. However, at
the time of the survey, eight of these states indicated that they still had some number of deaths under investigation. Extensive investigative procedures and the increasing use of formal death review teams to examine all of the evidence pertain-
ing to these cases has resulted in formal confirmation occurring several months,
and in some cases years, after a child has died. Consequently, we believe the actual number of deaths for 1997 will increase as more of these investigations are
completed. For these reasons, these data should be viewed as estimated. . . .

According to information from at least 16 states, 41% of the children who
died between 1995 and 1997 had prior or current contact with CPS agencies.
This substantial percentage may reflect the fact that many states only investigate deaths of children with current or prior CPS contact, thereby ensuring
that a high percentage of the reported deaths will involve such children. On
the other hand, the inability of child welfare agencies to provide sufficient services to all victims or to conduct comprehensive investigations of all reports
most likely contribute to this pattern. At least 20 states were able to report the
type of maltreatment which caused
the child's death. These percentages
remained fairly stable over the years.
Between 1995 and 1997, 44% died
from neglect, 51% died from abuse,
while 5% died as a result of multiple
forms of maltreatment. Young children remain at high risk for loss of
life. Based on data from all three
years, this study found that 78% of these children were under the age of five
while an alarming 38% were under the age of one at the time of their death.

> *"Although such deaths are
> relatively infrequent, the rate
> of child maltreatment fatalities
> confirmed by CPS agencies
> has risen steadily over the
> past eleven years."*

The ability of the child protection system to respond to the continued increase
in reports and child abuse fatalities largely depends on the resources available.
The amount of funding CPS agencies receive dictates whether reports get investigated, victims receive services or efforts are made to prevent maltreatment be-

fore a family enters the system. In this section, we investigate not only changes in child welfare budgets, but plans for spending future resources designed to prevent child abuse. . . .

Child abuse reports continue to climb at a steady rate despite the absence of significant new funding to states for investigation or service provision. In 1997, the number of child abuse reports rose 1.7%, exceeding 3.1 million. A similar increase in the number of substantiated cases also occurred, with over one million new cases entering child protective service caseloads last year. For the fourth consecutive year, the proportion of cases involving various forms of maltreatment were almost the same among the reported and substantiated cases, suggesting that a greater number of neglect cases and fewer child sexual abuse cases entered the system in 1997 as compared to in the 1980's and early 1990's. Of those cases that were substantiated, approximately 70% received some form of service.

> *"Child abuse reports continue to climb at a steady rate despite the absence of significant new funding to states for investigation or service provision."*

Although available data suggest a possible decrease in the total number of child abuse fatalities, the number of these cases continue to be disturbing. Looking across the past three years, 41% of these fatalities involved children who had current or prior contact with local child protective service agencies. The vast majority of these cases (78%) involved children under the age of five and more than one third were under the age of one (38%). Despite the increased implementation of child death review committees and administrative attention to the issue of child abuse fatalities, it is not certain that a consistent and meaningful decline in this issue is being realized.

While 56% of the respondents indicated that their agency had experienced increased state funding between 1996 and 1997, these increases were relatively small and may well be offset by the decline in funding expected from Federal sources. Further, changes in welfare policy at both the Federal and state levels are expected to have impacts on both the number of families in need of supportive services as well as on the overall rate of maltreatment.

Child Sexual Abuse Is a Widespread Problem

by Andrew Vachss

About the author: *Andrew Vachss has been an attorney and consultant in New York City since 1976. His individual practice is limited to the following matters concerning children and youth: abuse/neglect, delinquency, custody/visitation, and related tort litigation. His former specializations include juvenile defense, parole, and pre-sentence.*

Some people will tell you that there was no such thing as child sexual abuse a few short decades ago—the "good old days." And if you go to the files and read the old newspapers, you might well believe them.

Unless you were a victim, now grown to adulthood.

Then the media "discovered" child abuse. Like a pendulum, press coverage swung from one extreme to the other. From being reported so rarely that many doubted its very existence, child abuse became such a frequent subject of coverage that rarely a day went by without new accounts of horrors.

Now the media spotlight has been turned on defendants who maintain that they have been falsely accused of sexually abusing children—and the media backlash is so strong that you might well believe that we are in the midst of a modern-day Salem witch hunt.

Here's the truth: The battle against child sexual abuse is no "witch hunt." In Salem, there *were* no witches. In 20th-century America, sexual predators *do* exist—in alarming numbers.

Blaming the media won't make the problem go away. The media didn't invent child sexual abuse, and it can't make it disappear. Nor will our collective wishing make it do so. In fact, taking the ostrich approach actually benefits predators. Ignorance helps them to multiply, and cowardice makes them strong.

Facing the Truth

There are far more people who love and respect children than there are those who prey upon them. But if that is so, why aren't we winning this battle? Be-

Reprinted from Andrew Vachss, "If We Really Want to Protect Children," *Parade*, November 3, 1996. Reprinted with permission from the author (www.vachss.com).

cause, with all the media muddle surrounding child abuse, we are losing confidence in our collective ability to find out the truth.

How do we learn that truth? How do we protect our children?

A child abuse case is never a level playing field. It is never a fair fight. Why? What is so special about children that we treat these cases differently from other vicious crimes? Is it true that children's "memories" are different from those of adults? That children are easily "brainwashed" or cannot distinguish between truth and fantasy? Or is it that children are perceived as property, as lesser citizens, because of their age? Do we fear the inadequacy of their memories—or the truth of them?

I have never yet met an abused child (of whatever age) who was not crying to be heard and to be believed, to be validated and (eventually) assured that there was nothing "special" about him or her that brought on the abuse—that the child was simply a "parent's" (or other predator's) target of opportunity.

Child abuse cases *are* different, in part because the stakes are so much

> *"The battle against child sexual abuse is no "witch hunt." In Salem, there were no witches. In 20th-century America, sexual predators do exist—in alarming numbers."*

higher. If an adult is the victim of a crime, even if the defendant is acquitted, the adult is as "free" as the perpetrator. But in a child abuse case, the consequences of an improper acquittal are often that the victim is returned to the abuser.

The major difference between child abuse cases and all others is this: Those who make the decisions—be they judges, juries, social workers, police officers or the general public—too often act as though the "issue" were on trial, not the facts. But child sexual abuse is not an "issue," like capital punishment or abortion or gun control. Child abuse is a fact—a hideous, foul fact that traumatizes our culture just as it traumatizes individual victims.

If we want the truth about child sexual abuse, there is just one thing we can do: Look only at the facts of each individual case. It is not a question of "believing" children, or of "believing" in "witch hunts" or "false allegations." It is, and always will be, a question of fact-finding.

It sounds cold-blooded to say this, but a wrongful conviction of child abuse can be reversed. The damage from a wrongful acquittal probably cannot. Unless and until we learn to judge, case-by-case—unless and until we work to create a climate in which the facts *will* be found—countless victims will continue to be doomed.

Protecting one's own children is a biological imperative—it is how our species sustains itself. When an animal fails to protect its babies, they do not survive. And so the negative characteristics of that unprotective parent are not carried forth into new generations.

But it doesn't work that way with human beings. Our minds have evolved ways to sustain ourselves even when we ignore our biological in Children can no longer rely on our "instincts" for protection. On tions can achieve that goal.

For *every* parent who violates the sacred trust every child represents, thousands committed not only to protecting their children but also to protecting *all* children. That desire is our highest calling. The actual expression of that desire defines the character of each individual. And we can only truly express such a desire with behavior—rhetoric won't get the job done.

Healthy, happy, productive children—children who evoke their maximum potential—are no accident. They are not some fortuitous result of randomly scattering seeds on unnourishing ground. No, such children are always a harvested blessing, deeply dependent on climate and care. We create that climate and that care; and its most precious, indispensable element is *safety.*

Calling children "our most precious resource" is easy. Treating them as such is the key to our species.

More cases of child sexual abuse are *never* reported than are *ever* tried. Yes, some people are wrongfully convicted. And we must do our best to see that this never happens and to rectify it when it does. But no child benefits from being forced to carry the banner of a false allegation. Being made to do so is, in itself, a pernicious form of child abuse. And, every day, innocent victims are being ignored even when their cases do come to court.

What happens to those children?

Your children, America.

The Need for Adequate Resources to Fight Child Abuse

We need to pay what it costs to find the truth, because we can't afford what it costs not to. The best—indeed, the *only*—way to protect our children is to increase radically the resources available. We need therapy for all children who are the subject of child abuse allegations, regardless of any jury voting "guilty" or "not guilty."

We need better investigations. That means better investigators. And that means comprehensive training. It means adequate pay, competent supervision and full accountability. It means the use of standardized protocols, so that the outcome depends on the facts, not on the individual perspective of the investigator.

> *"Do we fear the inadequacy of [children's] memories— or the truth of them?"*

We need an objective "one-stop shop" system to avoid the confusion that results from subjecting a child to a series of interviews. All cases would be referred to a multidisciplinary resource center which has no vested interest in the outcome and which has the sole job of finding the facts. No party to the case—be it prosecution, defense, a parent in a custody battle or otherwise—would be permitted to control the investigation.

A full and complete record should be made available to all once it is finished.

For children especially, investigative interviewing to determine the likelihood of sexual abuse is an inherently intrusive and often traumatic experience. Because they want the pain to stop, many children go "mute" or "stop remembering," making it appear that they are changing their account of the events. And any such disparities can easily be exploited.

We need a system in which only wrongdoers fear the consequences.

It took an informed and enraged nation to pass child labor laws. It will take no less to protect children from an even more horrific societal crime.

We humans have been on the planet a long time. If we forget where we come from, if we forget our own children, then our evolution is not "in progress"—it is finished.

Child Abuse Fatalities Are Undercounted

by Nancy Lewis

About the author: *Nancy Lewis is a staff writer for the* Washington Post.

Even today, six years later, D.C. police Sgt. Bruce Feirson recalls every detail of the case of Chaulette Willis. The call that hot August afternoon came for an address in Southeast Washington that he knew well—a crack house and heroin shooting gallery. When he and paramedics arrived, they found not an adult drug victim but a tiny 4-month-old girl.

She was dirty and reeked of an awful odor, police and medical records show. The skin beneath her unchanged diaper was raw, ulcerated, rotting. The stench in the basement apartment was almost overwhelming. Doctors found two pounds of feces in the diaper of the 10-pound baby.

Chaulette was dead on arrival at the hospital; in fact, she may have been dead for 12 hours. The D.C. medical examiner blamed sudden infant death syndrome (SIDS)—usually used in an unexplained death in an otherwise healthy infant. No criminal investigation. Case closed.

"We find babies dead in horrible conditions here in [the 7th Police District] all the time," Feirson said, "and they're always coming back 'undetermined' . . . and nothing ever happens."

Undetermined Causes?

Chaulette's is one of 263 young children's deaths in the Washington area in recent years attributed to SIDS or "undetermined" causes. Scores more have been blamed on falls from sofas and beds and down stairs, accidental drownings and unexplained convulsions.

But dozens of these children likely were killed, either directly at the hand of another person or as the inevitable result of abuse or neglect, *The Washington Post* has found.

To try to gauge the true toll of this violence, *The Post* compiled death statistics, asked an expert to analyze them and interviewed police officers, prosecutors, doctors, child abuse experts and social workers from across the country and throughout the metropolitan area. All said they are certain numerous suspicious child deaths in the Washington region have gone undetected or been ignored.

The questions raised in the course of this reporting already have led the newly appointed D.C. chief medical examiner, Jonathan L. Arden, to reopen medical investigations into the causes of death for five children, including Chaulette, to determine whether they were homicides.

"There is a lot more child abuse than people think there is, and child abusers are not stereotypical but cross all economic and ethnic lines," said Craig Futterman, associate director of pediatric intensive care at Inova Hospital for Children in Fairfax County, one of the area's two main pediatric trauma centers. Throughout the region, children's deaths have been misexamined, mislabeled or misdiagnosed, according to interviews and a detailed review of child death statistics.

Doctors and medical examiners missed signs of injury, and the Washington area lacks the type of broad-based specialty teams that operate elsewhere in the country to immediately investigate children's deaths. Police investigations were poorly handled. Family members shielded accused relatives. And the bureaucracies assigned to flag cases of suspected abuse—from hospitals to schools to social service agencies—failed to respond.

"There is a lot more child abuse than people think there is."

Even in those area cases in which an adult was held accountable, punishment at times was minimal. In 1996 alone, a Silver Spring father punched and shook his 7-month-old and left him in a coma, a D.C. mother withheld medical care from her cancer-ridden son, and a Carroll County mother stuffed a rag into her 4-month-old daughter's mouth to quiet her. All three children eventually died. All three parents got suspended jail sentences or probation.

From scaldings to starvations to suffocations, there have been some child killings that generated public uproar, but most others passed without notice.

"All taken together, we are missing a substantial number of homicides," said Deputy Attorney General Eric H. Holder Jr., a former judge and former U.S. attorney for the District of Columbia.

The Hidden Death Toll

No single local or regional agency gathers statistics on child deaths in the Washington area. To learn how many children may have died from abuse and neglect here, *The Post* created a database of causes of death for the 2,379 area children younger than 5 who died from 1993 through 1995, the most recent year when complete information was available.

Of the 790 on average who died annually from all causes, only a few were officially recorded by police as homicides: 14 in 1993, five in 1994 and 10 in 1995.

Bernard Ewigman, a family practice physician and researcher in epidemiology at the University of Missouri-Columbia, analyzed the death data at *The Post*'s request. Ewigman and his research team have devised a mathematical formula for estimating how many childhood deaths attributed to "external causes"—which include anything that is not a disease or a condition the child had at birth—are in fact attributable to abuse or neglect. The method evolved from a landmark study the team published in 1993 in which it did intensive case-by-case studies of every child death in Missouri attributed to external causes during a six-year period and determined whether the original finding was correct.

> *"Fatal maltreatment is quite common—a phenomenon that is difficult to comprehend, much less accept, for most people."*

In examining the statistics for the Washington area, Ewigman said a conservative estimate is that a child a week in the region—50 each year—died from abuse or neglect, far more than in official police counts or court cases.

"True accidents are rare," Ewigman said. "Fatal maltreatment is quite common—a phenomenon that is difficult to comprehend, much less accept, for most people."

Collective Denial

Ewigman's method makes no attempt to unmask childhood deaths that had been attributed to natural causes but were, in fact, intentional killings. Neither Ewigman's team, nor anyone else, has tried to ferret out those cases from all the childhood deaths in a given area over a long period of time.

"Of course there are deaths signed out as SIDS or natural causes that are actually caused by child abuse, and there are even more that are caused by neglect, from starvation, failure to seek medical attention, failure to provide a safe environment," said Carole Jenny, director of the Child Protection Team at Hasbro Children's Hospital of Brown University in Providence, Rhode Island. Jenny has worked as a consultant to review autopsy results and medical reports in several child death cases in this area.

Several other national and local experts, including Arden, the District's new medical examiner, reviewed *The Post*'s database or the portions related to their expertise. All said they, too, believe an estimate of 50 abuse and neglect deaths in the region, although four to five times more than the official homicide numbers for several years, is conservative.

Futterman, who serves on the committee that reviews the circumstances of all child deaths in Fairfax County, estimates that 20 percent of all child deaths in the county—or 15 to 20 deaths a year in recent years—result from neglect or abuse. Those cases, Futterman said, can range from a fatal beating to fatal injuries that stem from a child's not being in a safety restraint at the time of a car accident.

Nationally, medical professionals have conducted at least three detailed studies of children's deaths from external causes over the last two decades. Each, using data from such differing locales as Chicago, New York City and Missouri, has found that deaths from maltreatment have been underreported by at least 50 percent.

Doing a better job overall of identifying the true cause of child deaths, Futterman said, would require that "kids have to matter in ways that right now they really don't."

It would also demand a willingness to suspect the possibility of killings that are almost too horrible to consider.

"The idea that parents or people close to a child could possibly injure or kill a child is just so abhorrent" that the possibility is often ignored, said Robert M. Reece, a Boston pediatrician and editor of the primary medical textbook on the diagnosis and treatment of abused or neglected children. "We are in collective denial."

Clusters of Deaths

The death data for the District and 17 surrounding jurisdictions point to clusters of deaths that demand more explanation.

In 1994 in the District, the percentage of young children's deaths attributed to an "undetermined" cause was 12.4 percent of all deaths—five times the 2.4 percent nationally for the same category.

The D.C. police department is the de facto clearinghouse for all suspicious child death information in the District, including those children who die at Children's Hospital, regardless of where their injuries occurred. Likewise, the D.C. medical examiner's office performs the autopsies for all those children.

> **"Deaths from maltreatment have been underreported by at least 50 percent."**

A special review of child deaths by the D.C. police homicide unit in late 1996 uncovered 92 cases in 1995 and 1996—half were children younger than 1—for which the medical examiner's office forwarded no final cause of death. In more than one-third of the deaths, 34, the preliminary findings stated that the cause of death was "undetermined."

Arden said that for the District to have more infants dying from unknown causes, which he described as a "wastebasket category," than from SIDS "begs for an explanation" and "raises the question of undetected smotherings."

Arden initiated a review of the 34 cases. In 14, records were missing or incomplete. Of the rest, 16 died from natural causes, one was correctly listed as undetermined, and three are now under active review as possible homicides, Arden said. He declined to identify those children.

Ebony Brown

Chaulette Willis was not on that list of 34, nor was Ebony Brown, whose case Arden reviewed at *The Post*'s request and has now reopened to determine whether the original stated cause of death is correct.

Like Chaulette, Ebony was born prematurely and drug-addicted, medical records show, weighing but 3 pounds, 13 ounces. She didn't leave the hospital until she was 7 weeks old and soon was hospitalized again for a severe diaper rash and a viral infection. But by Sept. 15, 1994, when she was 2 months old and sent home from the hospital again, she was up to 6 pounds, 9 ounces.

> *"The D.C. police homicide unit in late 1996 uncovered 92 [child deaths] in 1995 and 1996 ... for which the medical examiner's office forwarded no final cause of death."*

Eight weeks later, Ebony was dead.

Her mother told police that she found Ebony unconscious about 8:45 a.m. that Saturday in November. A doctor at Children's Hospital pronounced her dead 45 minutes later. An autopsy found numerous healed and healing fractures, including four fractured ribs and a broken bone in her arm. She also had multiple scrapes on her tiny body and severe diaper rash. She weighed just seven pounds. In two months, she had gained less than a half pound.

The D.C. medical examiner's office ruled at that time that the cause of Ebony's death was undetermined. No criminal investigation.

Chaulette's parents and Ebony's mother could not be located for comment on their daughters' deaths.

Several medical specialists who reviewed *The Post* data, saw questionable patterns in other death categories.

In Prince George's County in 1994, 11 percent of all deaths of children younger than 5 were attributed to "other newborn respiratory diseases," another red-flag category, those national experts said. Only 2.4 percent of child deaths nationwide fell in that category. The county also accounted for most of the deaths attributed to that cause for all of Maryland in 1994 and 1995.

Without delving into its old cases individually, the Prince George's County Health Department said it could not comment on those newborns' deaths. The Maryland medical examiner's office declined to comment, referring questions to the county.

Questionable SIDS Deaths

To get a picture of SIDS deaths, a category that has come under increased suspicion in recent years, *The Post* broadened its database to include causes of death for the 4,598 children younger than 5 from the District, Maryland and Virginia who died from 1992 through 1995.

In 35 rural Virginia counties and cities over a period of four years, there were 53 cases of SIDS deaths for children from age 28 days through 5 months, ᵢncluding some counties where every death of infants for that multi-year period was listed as a SIDS case and other counties where SIDS was the only cause listed for that age group in several of the years. Most of those counties are in rural areas, clustered in the Appalachian Mountains, the area between Petersburg and the North Carolina line, and along the Eastern Shore and the Chesapeake Bay.

Since 1993, Virginia law has required an autopsy be performed before a death can be attributed to SIDS, and that requirement, said Virginia's chief medical examiner, Marcella Fierro, leaves her confident of the SIDS findings in the clusters. "There are no child abuse deaths in those areas," Fierro said.

> "If the medics and police who respond to the call for help don't ask the right questions . . . a doubt may never be raised about a child's death."

In addition to an autopsy—which likely would not distinguish a SIDS death from a smothering—the American Academy of Pediatrics recommends an extensive battery of testing and a detailed investigation, including visiting the scene at which a child was found, before making a SIDS determination. A site visit could reveal discrepancies in accounts of the incident or other evidence that would point to a different cause of death.

Both the National Center for Health Statistics and the World Health Organization have agreed that no death should be ruled as SIDS without the death investigation the pediatrics group laid out. Virginia, Fierro said, is "largely relying" on testing recommended by the Armed Forces Institute of Pathology, which does not require a site visit.

One cluster of deaths currently recorded as accidental involves children suffocated by adults who may have been drunk or using drugs and in their sleep roll over on a child. Such deaths occur throughout the area, with two such fatal incidents in the District alone within a three-week period this summer.

Ryan A. Rainey, an assistant U.S. attorney in the District who for a decade has specialized in child homicide cases here and elsewhere, said prosecutors are looking for a test case to try to show that suffocations amount to a criminal act when they result from an adult's use of illegal drugs or from alcohol abuse.

"What's the difference between suffocating a baby while on drugs or intoxicated and getting behind the wheel of a car while on drugs or intoxicated and killing someone?" Rainey asked.

Confronting the Unthinkable

If the medics and police who respond to the call for help don't ask the right questions, if the doctors who treat the child don't realize the injuries couldn't fit the explanations offered, if the medical examiner assigned the case doesn't know what clues to look for, if relatives never share their disquiet, a doubt may never be raised about a child's death.

Even when the unthinkable becomes undeniable, a child's killer may never face any consequences.

Two years ago, a 4-month-old District girl was found dead in bed, and her death preliminarily was attributed to SIDS. When toxicology tests were completed months later, the true cause of death was found to be alcohol poisoning. A District police detective was then sent back to the home, but she said there were too many people sharing it for her to determine who might have fed alcohol to the child. No one has been charged in the case.

A year ago, 14-month-old Devon McCallister, an otherwise healthy boy, an autopsy shows, was found unconscious by his father in his babysitter's apartment on 12th Street in Southeast Washington just after midnight. He was pronounced dead at D.C. General Hospital. An autopsy showed he died of morphine poisoning.

Throughout the day, according to police, Devon had been in the care only of the family and the sitter. No one has been charged in his case.

The autopsy of 8-month-old Alonzo Rajah, who died in 1996 in the District, revealed that he had died of a fractured skull and indicated that a AA battery found lodged in his throat may have been inserted after death. Alonzo's death was ruled a homicide, but his killer has not been found.

It was a second child's killing that raised questions anew about a District child's death that had been ruled an accident.

Accidental Deaths?

When Monica Wheeler's battered body was found in the bathroom of the apartment of her mother's boyfriend in September 1997, D.C. paramedics immediately suspected that the 4-year-old had been beaten to death. An autopsy confirmed that, and her death was ruled a homicide. The boyfriend, Michael Lorenzo Tubman, 33, was charged.

Her killing came almost exactly three years after her brother, Andre Wheeler, 2, was found drowned with bruises on his head and neck—also while in the care of Tubman, who at the time gave various accounts of what had happened. The police homicide investigation of Andre's death ended when the medical examiner ruled it accidental. But after his sister's killing, it was reclassified—as a homicide.

> *"The younger the child, the easier it is to murder a child, and get away with it."*

Tubman denies killing Andre. When he pleaded guilty to manslaughter in Monica's death, he asked for leniency, blaming Monica's death on his "flipping" out on drugs. Without comment, D.C. Superior Court Judge Mary Ellen Abrecht sent him to prison for the maximum term allowable: 10 to 30 years on the manslaughter charge and 40 months to 10 years on the child abuse count, to run consecutively.

Prosecutors have decided not to pursue a homicide trial in Andre's death because the medical examiner's conflicting rulings undermine the case.

Doctors, police and prosecutors struggle with the emotional toll child death cases exact.

Assistant U.S. Attorney June M. Jeffries, who handles many of the child death cases that reach court in the District, said her work can be "a rather surreal world" in which she may attend a child's autopsy, then be obliged to carry on with routine appointments.

"I feel that you should be screaming, 'This baby is dead.' And instead, we have to go to lunch."

To Bill Hammond, who conducts training sessions nationally for the U.S. Justice Department in how to investigate children's deaths, there is a sad, disturbing truth about child killings.

Too often, he said, there never is a suspicion raised, and a child's passing is forever recorded as the unfortunate consequence of disease or accident.

"The younger the child, the easier it is to murder a child, and get away with it," Hammond said.

The Prevalence of Child Abuse Is Exaggerated

by Douglas J. Besharov and Jacob W. Dembosky

About the authors: *Douglas J. Besharov is a visiting professor at the University of Maryland's School of Public Affairs. He is the author of* Recognizing Child Abuse: A Guide for the Concerned. *Jacob W. Dembosky is a research assistant at the University of Maryland's School of Public Affairs.*

With a new government-funded study in hand, Secretary of Health and Human Services Donna Shalala diagnosed a rising epidemic of child abuse in September 1996. She reported that "child abuse and neglect nearly doubled in the United States between 1986 and 1993"—and that was only the beginning of the ugly news. The number of "serious" cases had quadrupled, and the percentage of cases being investigated by the authorities had actually *declined* by 36 percent, trends that she called "shameful and startling."

Is Shalala right? Is an unheeded child-abuse epidemic raging in America? Or, as I think is more likely, is the methodology behind the study and the interpretation of its numbers flawed? And if Shalala overstated the child-abuse peril, is she undermining public interest in the problem by making it appear too big and difficult to fix at a reasonable cost?

The secretary drew her statistics from the National Incidence Study of Child Abuse and Neglect, which was conducted by Westat Inc., a consulting firm that conducted similar studies in 1980 and 1986. In the new study, about 5,600 professionals, a representative sample, were asked by Westat whether the children they had served appeared to have suffered specified harms or to be living under specified conditions. Westat then determined if the reported "harms" and "conditions" met the study's definitions of "abuse" and "neglect," and generated estimates of incidence.

The odd thing about Shalala's claim that the number of children abused and neglected doubled from 1.4 million in 1986 to 2.8 million in 1993 is that no other signs point to such a dramatic increase in child abuse and neglect.

Reprinted from Douglas J. Besharov and Jacob W. Dembosky, "Child Abuse: Threat or Menace? How Common Is It Really?" October 3, 1996, available at www.slate.com/HeyWait/96-10-03/HetWait.asp. Reprinted with permission from Douglas J. Besharov.

Fatalities arising from child abuse have held roughly steady, ranging from 1,014 in 1986 to 1,216 in 1993, according to the National Committee to Prevent Child Abuse.

Of the 1.4 million additional cases reported, almost 80 percent fall into three suspect categories. (Anywhere from 13 percent to 34 percent of the 2.8 million children suffered more than one type of abuse or neglect. Unfortunately, the study did not "unduplicate" these reports. Nevertheless, the proportions I describe below provide a general picture of what is happening.)

Endangered children account for 55 percent of the increase. These are cases where the child was not actually harmed by parental abuse or neglect, but was "*in danger of being harmed* according to the views of community professionals or child-protective service agencies" [emphasis added].

Emotional abuse and neglect account for another 15 percent of the increase. The great majority of emotional-abuse cases, according to the 1986 Westat study, involved "verbal assaults," and more than half of the emotional-neglect cases involved "the refusal or delay of psychological care."

Educational neglect—the chronic failure to send a child to school—added another 8 percent to the total of new cases.

"Definitional Creep"?

All these cases warrant attention, but the explosion of numbers may be caused by the growing reportorial sensitivity of professionals, that is, "definitional creep." Professionals who become more sensitive to possible abuse, or more adept at noticing it, would make more reports to Westat—even if the actual incidence had not risen. In endangerment cases, at least, the study seems to accept this explanation.

According to Shalala, the number of "serious" cases increased between 1986 and 1993 from "about 143,000 to nearly 570,000." Her comments left the impression that the cases involved life-threatening assaults, but the study defines "serious" cases as any in which the child suffered "long-term impairment of physical, mental, or emotional capacities, or required professional treatment aimed at preventing such long-term impairment." Emotional maltreatment accounted for fully half of the increase in serious cases.

"Is an unheeded child-abuse epidemic raging in America?"

In cases labeled as serious physical abuse, the reported injury could be mental or emotional.

Even in these "serious" cases, the study seems affected by definitional creep. For example, in three categories (sexual abuse, physical neglect, and emotional neglect), the number of cases described as "moderate" declined even as the number of "serious" ones increased—strongly suggesting that cases once viewed as only moderately threatening have now been "upgraded" to the most dire category.

Chapter 1

Uninvestigated Cases?

Shalala's assertion that investigations of child abuse and neglect cases have dropped by 36 percent deserves closer scrutiny. In producing the number of uninvestigated cases, the study compared the number of cases identified by professionals with those known to local agencies. Of the cases not investigated, 33 percent involved educational neglect.

The main flaw here is that most educational-neglect cases are handled by the schools; reports are made to protective agencies only when all else fails.

> *"All [child abuse] cases warrant attention, but the explosion of numbers may be caused by the growing reportorial sensitivity of professionals."*

Another 30 percent of uninvestigated cases involved emotional abuse and neglect. But child-protective agencies usually avoid these cases because they tend to involve subjective judgments, and there is little that a quasi-law-enforcement agency can do about them.

Definitional creep is clearly at play here, too. Professionals who are increasingly willing to identify situations as harmful aren't necessarily ready to equate them with the sort of abuse and neglect they are legally obliged to report. And even if they did report these instances, child-protective agencies would still be expected to screen them out.

Probably not. Radical action would be required if Shalala's figures were even roughly correct. But instead of proposing radical action when she released the report, she outlined modest steps that had long been planned and budgeted.

Having worked in the field for 30 years, I can testify firsthand that the problem of child abuse and neglect is real. But however well meant, exaggerating the severity of abuse endangers children. In the late '80s, for example, the nation was told that 375,000 drug-exposed babies were born each year; Washington policy-makers were immobilized by estimates that tens of billions of dollars were needed to protect these children. In fact, the true number was closer to 35,000, and a decade later, the government has yet to mount a meaningful program for the children of addicts.

Overstatement may also obscure genuinely worrisome findings. Some of the increases in sexual abuse, physical abuse, and physical neglect uncovered by Westat may well reflect a true deterioration of conditions in disorganized, poverty-stricken households. But Shalala paid scant attention to this possibility.

And to claim recklessly that too few cases are investigated is to play with fire. Child-protective agencies are already overwhelmed investigating about 2 million reports a year, two-thirds of which are dismissed as unfounded or inappropriate. For many in the field, the most pressing need is to discourage inappropriate reporting—not to blithely call for more.

False Allegations of Child Sexual Abuse Are a Serious Problem

by Rael Jean Isaac

About the author: *Rael Jean Isaac writes on public policy issues for* National Review.

On January 14, 1997, two hundred people gathered in Salem, Massachusetts, to commemorate the three-hundredth anniversary of the Day of Contrition, a day of fasting and remorse proclaimed by the Massachusetts Bay Colony for the public hysteria and judicial misconduct that had led to "great hardship brought upon innocent persons" in what have come to be known as the Salem witch trials. Among those present were many of the chief participants in the struggle against their modern variant, the child-sex abuse persecutions of the 1980s and 1990s, most of which have included charges of Satanic ritual.

Ridiculous Charges

In addition to the pioneering researchers on the suggestibility of children and a handful of journalists who had kept their heads while their colleagues wallowed in sensation, there were the victims themselves. Kelly Michaels was there, the young would-be actress who served 5 years of a 47-year sentence on patently ridiculous charges of sexually molesting virtually all the 3- to 5-year-olds at the Wee Care Day Nursery unnoticed by any of her fellow workers. A prize moment from the trial: a child describes being forced to push a sword into Miss Michaels's rectum and being politely told "thank you" when he pulls it out. Also present were Peggy Ann and Ray Buckey, accused in the Mc-Martin case, the costliest criminal trial in U.S. history; Pastor Roberson and his wife, who supposedly turned their Baptist church in Wenatchee, Washington, into a site for mass sex orgies; Brenda and Scott Kniffen, who were each sentenced to 240 years in prison (and served 14 before their sentences were overturned) for participating in a nonexistent sex ring in Bakersfield, California; Violet and Cheryl Amirault, the mother and daughter who ran the Fells Acre nursery in Massachusetts, free after 7 years in prison, their sentences tossed out by an appeals-court judge.

While the presence in Salem of victims in some of the most high-profile cases suggested that the legal system was finally working, what their presence really pointed up was an anomaly: while appeals courts were throwing out the convictions of some of those unjustly imprisoned, they were arbitrarily denying so much as a hearing to others. Indeed, many were sinking ever deeper into the legal quagmire of their multiple life sentences.

Take the case of police officer Grant Snowden, North Miami Officer of the Year in 1983, who has now served 11 years of his five life sentences. He is one of several victims of false prosecutions for child sexual abuse ruthlessly pressed by Janet Reno when she was Dade County District Attorney (DA), prosecutions which catapulted her from obscurity into a national champion of children.

Snowden's ordeal began in the summer of 1984. His wife, Janice, had provided day care in their home for 15 years. She became concerned when 3-year-old Greg Wilkes, whom she had cared for since he was an infant, arrived at the house several times with welts that suggested he had been beaten. (Greg Wilkes and all the other names of children used here are the pseudonyms employed in the court records to protect the children's identity.) Snowden confronted the parents, telling them he would report them to the child-welfare authorities if Greg appeared like that again. Greg's vengeful father struck first, accusing Snowden of sexually molesting the child.

In the end, even Miss Reno did not have the stomach to press charges in this case. The father's manipulation of his son was so blatant that the psychiatrist who examined Greg warned his father to stop pressuring him to say things he did not want to say, and the case was dropped. But this only spurred the DA's office to greater efforts. With frantic parents now questioning children, a potential new complainant was found, 11-year-old Carol Banks, who claimed to have "recovered" memories of abuse at the Snowden home seven years earlier. Janet Reno brought in the heavy guns in the form of self-styled child-abuse experts Laurie and Joseph Braga (she had a PhD in speech, he in education). After a Braga interview had elicited a variety of charges from Carol, the prosecution felt ready to proceed to trial, but, as it turned out, miscalculated. Snowden was acquitted on all charges.

> *"While appeals courts were throwing out the convictions of some of those unjustly imprisoned, they were arbitrarily denying so much as a hearing to others."*

Undeterred, Miss Reno's office made good on a promise made to Snowden during the trial—to try him one child at a time until there was a conviction. On round three, the prosecution scored. This time there were two alleged victims, 4-year-old Leslie Blands and her 6-month-old brother. The case rested on Leslie's allegations. Yet New York attorney Robert Rosenthal points out in his brief seeking to overturn Snowden's conviction, "every single sexual comment and allegation made by Leslie was first suggested to her by Braga." This can be determined because the Bragas, like many of the early sex-abuse therapists proud of their techniques, videotaped their interviews.

The videotapes make plain that the Bragas used what analysts of these therapists' methods define as the standard techniques: repeated questioning in interview after interview when initial efforts receive the usual, "Nothing happened"; seeking only confirming evidence, avoiding paths that produce negative or inconsistent statements; setting an emotional tone in which parents and therapists will be proud if the child "helps," i.e., "tells"; asking the child to "pretend," then tell "what really happened," and then to "pretend" again until the child is totally confused; telling a child of allegations made by "other" children; and using so-called anatomically detailed dolls.

> *"Give a child . . . [a doll] with wide open mouth, anus, and vagina; the child will inevitably place one or more fingers in one of these conspicuous orifices."*

As Dr. Richard Gardner has pointed out, the dolls, with their disproportionately large genitals, are a terrible contaminant. Notes Gardner: "If one gives a child a peg and a hole, the child is going to put the peg in the hole. . . . Give a child one of these female anatomical dolls with wide open mouth, anus, and vagina; the child will inevitably place one or more fingers in one of these conspicuous orifices. For many of these workers, such an act is 'proof' that the child has indeed been sexually abused."

Although Leslie was not even able to identify Snowden in court, the judge surmounted this problem by permitting two other children to testify he had abused them (one was Greg Wilkes, now sufficiently coached; the second, another Braga product). But the judge forbade testimony about Snowden's exemplary record or that the Wilkes charges had been thrown out earlier or that Snowden had been tried and the jury had come in with a verdict of "not guilty" in the Banks case. The judge permitted the prosecutor's medical expert to introduce testimony that Leslie had tested positive for garderella vaginitis but refused to allow the defense medical expert, Dr. Max Bertholf, to point out that the test used was a sloppy one, at best no more than 50 per cent accurate. The jury was not even allowed to hear that the prosecution's doctor had herself now discarded the test because of its inaccuracy.

A No-Win Situation

And so it went. When Leslie partly recanted under insistent questioning by Snowden's attorney, Joseph Braga took the stand to accuse the attorney of child abuse and to explain that such withdrawals were "typical" of abused children. Here indeed was a no-win situation—if the child accused the defendant, he was guilty, and if the child recanted, it was further evidence he was guilty.

> *"If the child accused the defendant, he was guilty, and if the child recanted, it was further evidence he was guilty."*

Despite the egregious errors in the trial, appeals courts have turned a deaf ear. In 1989 the Florida Court of Appeal agreed to "comment" only on the issue of whether Snowden had in effect wound up being convicted for what he supposedly did to the other two children, when he was not on trial for abusing them. The court solemnly concluded that "less than one-half of the witnesses and only one-third of the testimony" were devoted to them. By the mid 1990s Snowden had exhausted all possibility of appeal in state courts; Rosenthal, along with attorney Arthur Cohen, is now seeking to win a hearing in federal court [in 1998, a federal court overturned Snowden's conviction]. The Florida attorney general has already moved three times to strike their brief, on the ground that they are procedurally barred from raising each and every issue.

Outrageous as the Snowden case is, it was not Janet Reno's worst child-sex-abuse prosecution. That accolade goes to her most famous case, known as Country Walk, after the upscale suburban-Miami development in which it unfolded. This time day care was provided by newlywed 17-year-old Ileana Fuster, seeking to supplement the income of her 36-year-old husband Frank's decorating business. There was a mother's suspicion to light the fuse: picking up her 18-month-old, awakened from sleep and groggy, the mother decided he had been drugged. And there were the Bragas to elicit the requisite charges from 2- to 4-year-olds. (The oldest child was 5.) Sample: "They'd pee in something, put slime in it, put punch in, mix it up, put caca and turtle skins in, and everybody would drink it."

But what makes Rosenthal call this case "the worst I have ever seen" is the brutality with which Miss Reno's office wrested a confession from Ileana Fuster, scarcely more than a child herself. In a sworn deposition, Stephen Dinerstein, the experienced investigator employed by the Fusters' attorneys, described the conditions in which Ileana was held and their effect on her. She had been a bright, attractive girl with shiny black hair; now she "appeared as if she was 50 years old. Her skin was drawn from a large loss of weight. . . . She has sores and infections on her skin and states that no sanitary conditions exist or are provided, that the shower, when received, is a hosing down in the cell. That she is in a cell with nothing in it but a light in the ceiling and that she is often kept nude and in view of everybody and anybody." As a result of her mistreatment, said Dinerstein, she had become "a constantly crying, shaking, tormented person who understands little if anything about the whole process and is now being threatened and promised and is totally in a state of confusion to the point of not having the slightest idea as to month and date."

Intimidation

None of this could have been lost on Miss Reno, for she repeatedly visited Ileana Fuster. Dinerstein reports that during the last two weeks of July 1985 (after 11 months, most of it in solitary confinement) "Mrs. Fuster's condition had deteriorated so badly she could hardly move and was very slow to respond to any questions. When asked if Mr. Van Zamft [her attorney] was present, she could not even recall, but said simply that the woman State Attorney [Reno] was very big and very scary and made suggestions as to problems that would arise if she didn't cooperate." How often Janet Reno personally came to apply the screws is uncertain. But whatever their number, those visits appall Robert Rosenthal. "I never heard of that before. I can't imagine that any state official should be coming to visit inmates, especially a weak young woman defendant in isolation, half the time medicated, her sleep cycles altered, hypnotized [by Michael Rappaport and Merry Lou Haber]." These were psychologists employed by Ileana's own attorney (who wanted her to plea bargain) to help her "recover" memories of abuse. To compound the psychological torture, people from Reno's office took her on rare trips to good Spanish restaurants to remind her of what life could be like if she cooperated.

Despite all the pressures upon her, Ileana steadfastly maintained her own and Frank's innocence for 11 months. But in the summer of 1985 she cracked. Wedged between Michael Rappaport and Janet Reno, whose hand she clutched, Ileana gave her deposition. What the children had said, she now testified, was true and then some: Frank had hung his own 6-year-old son, Noel, by the feet in the garage and twisted him like a punching bag; hung her up by her arms in the same garage; spread feces on her; forced her to perform sexual acts on the children at knifepoint; put snakes in her genitals and those of the children; and stuck a cross in her rectum. Reno assistant John Hogan, who prosecuted the case in the courtroom, described these and the other charges to the jury as "unimaginable acts" when they were, in point of fact, imaginary acts.

> *"That some of those falsely accused go free . . . and others remain to serve out life terms often constitutes no more than a legal lottery."*

As the reward for her cooperation, Ileana was sentenced to 10 years and after 3 was released and deported to Honduras. Frank was sentenced to six life terms plus 165 years.

Although Frank's appeals went nowhere, he almost won his freedom in 1995. Ileana gave a sworn 60-page deposition to attorney Arthur Cohen in Honduras, detailing the methods that had been used to coerce her into making a false confession. But now, said Ileana, ten years had gone by, her mind was clear, and she knew there had never been any abuse of children in her home. "I have no memories of that [abusing the children] because nothing really happened."

Chapter 1

Since Ileana refused to come back to the United States (a vindictive DA's office would have tried her for perjury for lying under oath at the first trial), Rosenthal and Cohen persuaded the judge to allow her to testify over satellite from Honduras. But within days of the scheduled hearing, Ileana had retracted her retraction via a letter to the Miami Herald. The bottom line was that she wanted to let her original deposition stand and wanted Frank's attorneys "to leave me alone, please."

> *"Of all the genuine child abuse in these cases . . . none compares to the coercion of small children to testify against their parents."*

What had happened? Rosenthal believes she was threatened by someone determined that Country Walk not unravel, and is sure she did not write the letter she signed.

But whatever happened, the door had now shut fast on Frank Fuster. According to Cohen and Rosenthal, his hopes for successful appeal are now all but lost. And while Fuster does not have Snowden's exemplary background (Fuster had served four years in New York for killing a man in a traffic dispute and at the time of Country Walk was on probation for touching a 9-year-old girl on the breast through her clothing) both men are imprisoned till death for crimes that not only did they not commit, but that never happened.

A Legal Lottery

That some of those falsely accused go free, their sentences finally reversed on appeal, and others remain to serve out life terms often constitutes no more than a legal lottery. *People v. Stoll* is a famous case and the term "Stoll's evidence" is now used to refer to the California Supreme Court's recognition of the right of those accused of bizarre sexual acts against children to introduce expert psychological evidence, including the results of recognized tests, as evidence that they do not fit the profile of sexual deviants. Most people who have heard of the case assume that Stoll won his freedom with it, but in fact, because of a technicality, it was the sentences of his two co-defendants, Timothy Palomo and Margie Grafton, that were overturned. Fourteen years into his life sentence, Stoll remains incarcerated. Now married, Grafton and Palomo are reunited with Margie Grafton's children, whose testimony had been key in convicting them.

Of all the genuine child abuse in these cases—committed by therapists, prosecutors, and families who manipulate children to bear false witness—none compares to the coercion of small children to testify against their parents, often with the false promise that as soon as they have told the therapists what they want to hear, they will be reunited with their family. Donna Hubbard's 9-year-old son Richie was coerced into testifying against her in the same Kern County hysteria over alleged interlocking Satanic sex rings that swallowed up Grafton, Palomo, and Stoll. He says that it was not until he was a teenager, cared for by a foster family who loved him, that he realized "my mom was in prison and I did it."

Sometimes the ordeal is not over even when it seems finally, mercifully, to be at an end. In April of 1997 the Massachusetts Supreme Judicial Court overruled the appellate judge, reinstating the convictions of Violet and Cheryl Amirault in the interests of achieving "finality." For Violet Amirault, at 74, prison would be finality indeed. (There has been a last-minute stay of execution. The Superior Court judge who was expected to carry out the decision of the Supreme Judicial Court instead defiantly ordered a new trial.) [Violet Amirault died of stomach cancer on September 12, 1997. Cheryl Amirault's request for a new trial was rejected by the Massachusetts Supreme Court on August 18, 1999. She has since been paroled. Gerald Amirault remains in prison.]

Apparently finality is a virtue only when it incarcerates. Prosecutors have been unwilling to close the door on the case that has made Edenton, North Carolina, internationally infamous, thanks to Ofra Bikel's brilliant documentaries on PBS's *Frontline*. In 1995, the North Carolina Supreme Court upheld the appellate decision that threw out the convictions of Little Rascals Day Care owner Robert Kelly (12 consecutive life sentences) and cook Dawn Wilson (merely one life sentence), the only two of the "Edenton 7" actually to go before a jury. (Sample allegations by the children: they were taken aboard a space ship and abused in outer space; "Mr Bob" [Kelly] killed babies with a gun; abused on a ship while trained sharks swam around the boat.) But in a case of vindictive prosecution, Assistant DA Nancy Lamb has conjured up a new, previously unknown supposed victim of Kelly's and is now pressing

> *"Since medical evidence is usually either wholly absent or amibiguous, the cases ultimately rest on the testimony of . . . very small children."*

forward. Bob Kelly has shown amazing grace through this ordeal. After six years in prison, he has lost everything, but still tithes his small salary as a telephone maintenance man.

Still, Kelly has been comparatively fortunate in that his case attracted international attention, forcing the appellate court to examine it closely. The same appeals court upheld the three consecutive life sentences of Patrick Figured, whose trial, held without fanfare, had been contemporaneous with that of Kelly. Yet public appellate defender Mark Montgomery, who represented both men, says that legally the case was even worse than Kelly's. Once the therapists were through with them, the children insisted "Pat" forced the dog to urinate and made them drink it, thrust candles and screwdrivers up their rectums, forced them to perform oral sex, and burned a Bible in a barrel while dressed up like the devil. Co-workers testified that Figured worked eight-to-five as a manufacturing manager at a job an hour's drive away from the day care center and was never absent from the office except for a lunch break. He would have had to fly on a broom to be present on some of the occasions when he was accused of inflicting his laundry list of Satanic crimes.

Chapter 1

No End in Sight

How many innocent people are currently serving long, often life sentences for sexual abuse of children? The situation in North Carolina suggests a significant national problem. Montgomery says that for the last ten years he has been almost exclusively engaged in appeals in sexual-abuse cases, around 250 in all. Asked how many of those convicted were innocent, Montgomery said he was unable to say. What he could say was that most trials were so poorly conducted, and the defendant's ability to mount a defense so limited, that an objective reader of the transcripts would say at the end of it, "Well, this guy might have done it, but we sure wouldn't know it from the trial."

Nor, after 14 years, is there any end in sight. Few people realize in how short a span the Salem witch hysteria flamed and then burnt itself out. It began in January 1692 when two girls began acting strangely and babbling incoherently; the trials started in March; the executions began in June (19 "witches" were hung and an additional victim pressed to death by rocks); in October the governor forbade further imprisonments for witchcraft. It was all over in 10 months—16 months if one postpones closure until the governor's order to release all accused "witches" remaining in jail. While the big Satanic-ritual-abuse cases are on the wane, the small cases march on, with the legal system showing little ability to separate valid from spurious claims.

In one very important respect, the situation has grown worse. Since medical evidence is usually either wholly absent or ambiguous, the cases ultimately rest on the testimony of children, often very small children. It thus becomes crucial to determine where that testimony comes from: Is the source the child or the therapist? Only if the therapist's interviews with the child are taped is it possible to tell. But precisely because videotapes have been vital to the defense, many prosecutors now seek to avoid them. At the trial of Patrick Figured psychologists Mark Everson and Barbara Boat both testified that the attorney general's office had "encouraged" them not to tape their interviews with the children. Wenatchee investigators actually destroyed their notes.

Systematic Injustice

For many the only hope for relief may lie in a governor's pardon. But governors are not going to act without public support. There has been no modern-day William Phips, the Massachusetts Bay Colony governor who emptied the jails of "witches." Terrified of being perceived as soft on child abuse, not a single governor has pardoned a single individual in any of these cases. The most any has done is try to pass the buck. In 1996, then-Governor Mike Lowry of Washington asked Janet Reno for a Justice Department investigation of civil-rights violations in Wenatchee, a ludicrous proposition given Miss Reno's record. (Needless to say, she refused to get involved.)

It is of vital concern to everyone that our legal system not be corrupted by systematic injustice. But thus far, these cases constitute a reverse morality tale.

43

Child Abuse

The innocent languish in prison while those who put them there prosper. Scott Harshbarger, prosecutor of the Amiraults, went on to become Massachusetts attorney general. And none have done as well as the prosecutors of Country Walk. Janet Reno rode her triumph in that case to become U.S. attorney general. John Hogan, who helped prosecute Country Walk, was rewarded with a plum newly created job as statewide prosecutor. In less than a year he was forced to resign when it transpired that he had bought "hot suits" from a man who was fencing men's clothing for a fourth the normal price from a private residence—all cash and no sales tax, making Hogan an unlikely "innocent victim," as he portrayed himself. Miss Reno then took her right-hand man back, and later brought him to Washington, where he currently serves as chief of staff at the Justice Department.

But if the wrongdoers have flourished, the American public has indirectly paid a heavy price. Within weeks of assuming her post, Janet Reno ordered the tanks into Waco [In 1993, after a fifty-one day standoff with federal authorities, eighty Branch Davidians were killed when fire engulfed their compound.], her decision, by her own account, precipitated by two words: "child abuse." Someone had told her the Branch Davidians were beating children, and although the Federal Bureau of Investigation (FBI) would later acknowledge the report was false, Miss Reno had not paused to inquire further. Among the 79 who died there, 25 were children. And Timothy McVeigh [who bombed the Alfred P. Murrah Building in Oklahoma City on April 19, 1995] was obsessed with avenging Waco.

Chapter 2

What Causes Child Abuse?

Chapter Preface

> I didn't have a family life. My mother used to sit on my head to make me still so she could beat me with a cord, belt, or anything she could get her hands on, and things got worse when she burned me with an iron, and she allowed certain relatives to have sex with me.

These are the words of "Alma," an abused child who would grow up to abuse her own son so severely that he would die of his injuries. Alma's story, quoted by Susan Crimmins and her coauthors in a study of women who have killed children, lends credence to the commonly held view that child abuse is passed on from generation to generation in a "cycle of violence." In short, the theory goes, people who are abused as children are more likely to abuse their own children later in life.

A study by Byron Egeland provides further support to this hypothesis. Egeland interviewed 47 mothers who were abused as children and found that 40 percent were currently mistreating their own children. By contrast, of 35 mothers who were not abused as children, only 9 percent were mistreating their children.

While strong evidence suggests that the tendency to abuse children is passed across generations, even Egeland concedes that an abused child will not automatically grow up to abuse his or her children. The majority (60 percent) of abused mothers in his study were not abusing their children. As Egeland states, "A history of abuse is a major risk factor for abusing, but it is not a guarantee that abuse will occur in the next generation. There are many additional risk factors that need to be considered." Perhaps the greatest of these risk factors is poverty. According to Alex Morales, the Executive Director of the Children's Bureau of Southern California, "Parents are 22 times more likely to abuse their offspring if they live on less than $15,000 annually than are those who earn more than $30,000 per year."

Other risk factors cited by experts include substance abuse in the home, family instability, and inefficient social service systems. These and other factors are the topic of the following chapter on the causes of child abuse.

Substance Abuse Is Responsible for Child Abuse

by Joseph A. Califano Jr.

About the author: *Joseph A. Califano Jr. is the chairman and president of the National Center on Addiction and Substance Abuse at Columbia University in New York City.*

A devastating tornado of substance abuse and addiction is tearing through the nation's child welfare and family court systems leaving in its path a wreckage of abused and neglected children, turning social welfare agencies and courts on their heads and uprooting the traditional disposition to keep children with their natural parents.

There is no safe haven for these abused and neglected children of drug- and alcohol-abusing parents. They are the most vulnerable and endangered individuals in America.

That is the grim finding of The National Center on Addiction and Substance Abuse at Columbia University's (CASA) two-year exhaustive analysis of the available data on child abuse and neglect; an unprecedented CASA national survey of 915 professionals working in the field of child welfare; a review of more than 800 professional articles, books and reports; six case studies of innovations in the field and numerous in-depth interviews with judges, child welfare officials and social workers on the frontlines.

The Damage Caused by Substance Abuse

From 1986 to 1997, the number of abused and neglected children in America has jumped from 1.4 million to some 3 million, a stunning rise more than eight times faster than the increase in the children's population (114.3 percent compared to 13.9 percent). The number of *reported* abused and neglected children that have been killed has climbed from 798 in 1985 to 1,185 in 1996; the U.S.

Advisory Board on Child Abuse and Neglect sets the actual number higher, at 2,000, a rate of more than five deaths a day.

Alcohol, crack cocaine, methamphetamine, heroin and marijuana are fueling this population explosion of battered and neglected children. Children whose parents abuse drugs and alcohol are almost three times (2.7) likelier to be physically or sexually assaulted and more than four times (4.2) likelier to be neglected than children of parents who are not substance abusers. With 28 million children of alcoholics and several million children of drug addicts and abusers, the number of children and adults in America who, during their lives, have been neglected and/or physically and sexually assaulted by substance-abusing parents is a significant portion of our population.

Parental neglect of children is a consequence of substance abuse and addiction and such neglect often leads to sexual or physical abuse by others. While three-fourths (77.8 percent) of abuse perpetrators are birth parents, 10.1 percent are other relatives and 12.1 percent are unrelated adults.

In 1998, CASA conducted the first survey about substance abuse and addiction ever undertaken of frontline professionals in child welfare agencies and family courts. The responding 915 professionals hail from every state, and from inner city, suburban and rural areas. This survey reveals a corps of professionals sounding the alarm and crying out for help. The picture of child abuse and neglect in America that they paint is colored with alcohol and drug abuse and addiction. Eight of 10 professionals surveyed (81.6 percent) cite alcohol in combination with other drugs as the leading substance of abuse in child abuse and neglect; another 7.7 percent cite alcohol alone; 45.8 percent cite crack cocaine as the leading illegal substance of abuse; 20.5 percent, marijuana. For these child welfare workers confronting parental maltreatment of children, marijuana can hardly be considered a benign substance.

> *"Alcohol, crack cocaine, methamphetamine, heroin and marijuana are fueling this population explosion of battered and neglected children."*

Eighty percent (79.8) of the professionals said that substance abuse causes or exacerbates most cases of child abuse and neglect that they face; 40 percent (39.7) reported that it causes or exacerbates 75 to 100 percent of their cases. So pervasive has drug and alcohol abuse been among parents receiving services of the Department of Health and Human Services in Sacramento County, California (notably including alcohol and methamphetamine use by child-abusing parents), that the department's former director Robert Caulk required every employee to receive intensive training in substance abuse and addiction.

The Financial and Human Costs of Substance Abuse

Although estimates vary, CASA's analysis, survey and interviews lead to the finding that parental substance abuse and addiction is the chief culprit in at least

70 percent—and perhaps 90 percent—of all child welfare spending. Using the more conservative 70 percent assessment, in 1998 substance abuse and addiction accounted for some $10 billion in federal, state and local government spending simply to maintain child welfare systems.

This $10 billion does not include the costs of providing healthcare to abused and neglected children, operating law enforcement and judicial systems consumed with this problem, treating developmental problems these children suffer, providing special education for them or lost productivity. Nor does it include the costs attributable to child abuse and neglect

> *"Parental neglect of children is a consequence of substance abuse and addiction and such neglect often leads to sexual or physical abuse by others."*

that are privately incurred. It has been impossible to calculate those costs with precision, but CASA estimates that they easily add an additional $10 billion to the price our nation and its people pay for child abuse and neglect.

The human costs are incalculable: broken families; children who are malnourished; babies who are neglected, beaten and sometimes killed by alcohol- and crack-addicted parents; eight-year-olds sent out to steal or buy drugs for addicted parents; sick children wallowing in unsanitary conditions; child victims of sodomy, rape and incest; children in such agony and despair that they themselves resort to drugs and alcohol for relief. For some of these children it may be possible to cauterize the bleeding, but the scars of drug- and alcohol-spawned parental abuse and neglect are likely to be permanent.

Parental substance abuse does not fester in a cocoon. It is usually found among a cluster of daunting conditions—poverty, a history of having been physically or sexually abused, depression, other mental illness, unemployment, discrimination and social isolation. The impact of poverty is profound: children from families with incomes below $15,000 are 25 times likelier to be abused and neglected than children from families with incomes above $30,000, and parents of poor children are less likely to have access to treatment. The parent who abuses drugs and alcohol is often a child who was abused by alcohol- and drug-abusing parents. Most parents involved with child welfare systems are women since so many men have walked out on their parental responsibilities.

An Overwhelmed System

This violent storm of parental drug and alcohol abuse and addiction has overwhelmed the dedicated army of more than 200,000 caseworkers, judges, lawyers and child advocates in the nation's 1,000 state, county and private child welfare agencies, 1,200 family courts and thousands of foster care and adoption agencies.

By 1997, in some states and cities caseworkers were responsible for 50 cases of child maltreatment at any one time and judges were handling as many as 50 cases a day. At that pace, in less than 10 minutes a judge must assess the circumstances and credibility of the mother and/or father, child, caseworker, siblings, law enforcement officer and any other witnesses and make a decision that may determine a child's future—and that assumes the judge is working on the substance of these cases for more than eight non-stop hours a day!

> *"Substance abuse and addiction has shaken the foundations of the nation's child welfare systems."*

Few caseworkers and judges who decide for these children have been tutored in substance abuse and addiction. While most child welfare officials say they have received some training, usually it involves brief, one-shot seminars that last as little as two hours. For judges, training tends to be on-the-job. Such training is woefully inadequate for the profound decisions that these officials are called upon to make for these vulnerable children.

Despite the sharp rise in cases of child abuse and neglect involving alcohol and drugs, the number of families receiving in-home services from caseworkers has dropped 58 percent, from 1.2 million in 1977 to 500,000 in 1994. In 1997, child welfare workers were able to investigate only a third (33 percent) of cases of child abuse and neglect, a decline from 1986 when they investigated half (51 percent) of such cases.

There are no national estimates of the gap between those parents who need treatment and those who receive it, but CASA's research concerning women and a study of 11 states indicates that most of those who need treatment don't receive it. Drug and alcohol addiction is a chronic disease so without treatment and aftercare, these parents have little hope of recovery.

Shifting Priorities

Substance abuse and addiction has shaken the foundations of the nation's child welfare systems and fundamentally changed the nature of the tasks required of the professionals involved. Physical and sexual abuse and neglect are striking younger and younger children and a growing number of babies. As the role of substance abuse has increased, the age of the victimized children has gone down. Many fetuses are exposed to alcohol, illegal drugs and tobacco during pregnancy: between 1991 and 1995, alcohol use during pregnancy rose more than 30 percent (from 12.4 to 16.3 percent of pregnant women). Each year, some 20,000 infants are abandoned at birth or are kept at hospitals to protect them from substance-abusing parents. The proportion of children that caseworkers place in foster care at birth jumped 44 percent from the 1983–86 period (16 percent) to the 1990–94 period (23 percent). Today most cases of abuse and neglect by substance-abusing parents involve children under five.

Generations ago, child welfare workers were able to concentrate on care of the children; for them, reconstituting the natural family was a happy result and it was often just a matter of getting an unemployed parent a job or helping husband and wife deal with an intense but passing personal crisis. Alcohol and drugs have blown away the topsoil of family life and reshaped the landscape of child abuse and neglect. Parents addicted to drugs and alcohol are clever at hiding their addiction and often more concerned about losing their access to drugs and being punished than losing custody of their children. As a result, child welfare agencies have been forced to allocate more time to investigations, gathering evidence of neglect and abuse of children by alcohol and drug involved parents that increasingly leads to criminal prosecution. This shift in focus has changed the way parents and children see caseworkers and the way these workers view themselves, immeasurably complicating their task of protecting children and either putting the birth family back together again or placing the child with another set of parents. This shift also threatens to criminalize a process that should be driven by treatment, healthcare and compassion for both child and parent.

A Threat to Family Preservation

Drug and alcohol abuse has thrown into doubt a fundamental tenet of child welfare: the commitment to keep the child with his or her natural parents. Child welfare workers have long viewed terminating parental rights as a failure. But alcohol, crack cocaine and other drug abuse has shattered this time-honored precept. Where drug- and alcohol-abusing and addicted parents are concerned, the failure often rests in perpetuating such rights at the expense of the child's development.

There is an irreconcilable clash between the rapidly ticking clock of cognitive and physical development for the abused and neglected child and the slow motion clock of recovery for the parent addicted to alcohol or drugs. In the earliest years, the clock of child development runs at supersonic speed—intellectually, physically, emotionally and spiritually. For the cognitive development of young children, weeks are windows of early life that can never be reopened. For the parent, recovery from drug or alcohol addiction takes time—certainly months and often years—and relapse, especially during initial periods of recovery, is common. Quick fixes and cold turkey turnarounds are the rare exception for alcohol and drug addicts and abusers. Bluntly put, the time that parents need to conquer their substance abuse and addiction can pose a serious threat to their children who may suffer permanent damage during this phase of rapid development. Little children cannot wait; they need safe and stable homes and nurturing adults *now* in order to set the stage for a healthy and productive life.

> *"Drug and alcohol abuse has thrown into doubt a fundamental tenet of child welfare: the commitment to keep the child with his or her natural parents."*

For some parents, concern about their children can provide a primary motiva-

51

tion to seek treatment for alcohol and drug abuse and addiction. But for many, the most insidious and horrifying aspect of substance abuse and addiction is its power to overwhelm and even destroy the inherent natural instinct of parents to love and care and sacrifice for their children. Whether the abuse involves alcohol, crack cocaine or some other drug, its most savage manifestation is the destruction of the motivation of parents to seek help for their addiction so that they can care for their children. Eighty-six (85.8) percent of survey respondents named lack of motivation as the number one barrier to getting parents into substance abuse treatment.

Children Pay the Price

The cruelest dimension of the tragedy for children abused by parents using drugs and alcohol is this: even if parental rights are timely terminated for such parents who refuse to enter treatment or who fail to recover, there is no assurance of a safe haven for the children. There are not nearly enough adoptive homes for these children. Some 107,000 children were either legally free or destined for adoption at the end of 1995; only 27,115 children—one in four— were adopted that year. Foster care, while far better than being abused, rarely offers the lasting and secure nurturing for full cognitive development—and appropriate foster care is also in short supply.

Child welfare professionals struggle with this problem. More than eight of 10 (82.4 percent) believe that repeated abuse should prompt termination of parental rights and three fourths (75.1 percent) believe that severe abuse requires such termination. Yet these professionals admit that in current practice, far fewer such cases result in termination.

Parental alcohol and drug abuse and addiction have thrown the nation's system of child welfare beyond crisis, into chaos and calamity. It is the children who pay the exorbitant price. They are beaten by mothers and fathers high on alcohol or cocaine. They are left to suffer malnutrition and disease because they lack food and heat. Children of substance-abusing parents suffer low self-esteem, depression, self-mutilation, suicide, panic attacks, truancy and sexual promiscuity, and in later life mimic the drug and alcohol abuse problems that they witness in their parents. For most of these children, we offer no safe port from the storm of parental drug and alcohol abuse and addiction that has engulfed their lives. We spend more on cosmetic surgery, hairpieces and make-up *for men* than we do on child welfare services for children of substance-abusing parents. In this nation, we take better care of endangered condors than of children of substance-abusing parents.

The best hope of a safe haven for these children is to prevent alcohol and drug abuse by their parents.

Child welfare systems and practices need a complete overhaul. Some leaders in the field have moved to reshape systems under their control. The former Director of the Sacramento County Department of Health and Human Services required all employees to be intensively trained in substance abuse and addiction. Officials in Connecticut and New Jersey have enlisted specialists in drug and alcohol addiction to screen and assess parents, place them with treatment providers and monitor their progress. Judges in Reno, Nevada, Pensacola, Florida, and Suffolk County, New York, have used their family courts to coerce parents into treatment and follow their progress closely, an innovation that is being replicated in other parts of the country.

Social service providers, from agency directors to frontline child welfare workers, judges, court clerks, masters, lawyers, and health and social service staffs need intensive training in the nature and detection of substance abuse, and what to do when they spot it. States should require as a condition of certification that child welfare workers be thoroughly trained in substance abuse and addiction and require these workers to undergo continuing education on the subject. In all investigations of child abuse or neglect, parents should be screened and assessed for substance abuse: those who need help should be offered comprehensive treatment. Caseworkers and judges should use the carrots and sticks at their disposal to get parents who need it into treatment and should prevent and plan for relapse. They should move rapidly to place children for adoption when parents refuse treatment or fail to respond to it.

Family Preservation Laws Put Children at Risk for Abuse

by Dennis Saffran

About the author: *Dennis Saffran is the executive director of the Center for the Community Interest, a national organization that serves as a voice for the community on crime and quality-of-life issues.*

On the day before Easter the mentally unstable mother of a five-year-old Bronx boy named Daytwon Bennett tied him to a chair and beat him to death with a broomstick. Starving when he died—he weighed just 30 pounds—Daytwon had suffered "multiple blunt impact injuries" over a long period, according to the autopsy report. Daytwon was not unknown to the child welfare authorities. They had removed him from his mother's custody and placed him in foster care on four separate occasions in his short lifetime—only to uproot him and send him back to her for more abuse each time.

Daytwon's killing was just the latest in a parade of tragedies in which children have been murdered or severely injured after judges and caseworkers have returned them to—or allowed them to remain with—violent, deranged, or drug-addicted parents. In November 1995, New York and the nation recoiled in horror at the death of six-year-old Elisa Izquierdo at the hands of her crack-addicted mother, who had regained custody of the girl despite the anguished pleas of her other relatives and preschool teachers.

That same month a Bronx judge ordered 17-month-old Rayvon Evans removed from the foster mother with whom he had always lived and returned to the drug-addicted and alcoholic mother who had abandoned him at birth. Three months later she scalded him to death, and two months after that, when the stench got too strong, her boyfriend tossed the decomposing body out the window into a dumpster.

A few months before Elisa died, the drug-addicted mother of a two-year-old

Reprinted from Dennis Saffran, "Fatal Preservation," *City Journal*, Summer 1997. Reprinted with permission from the Manhattan Institute.

Long Island boy punched him hard enough to rupture his intestines and kill him—because he would not stop crying. She had broken his arm on a previous visit, but social workers had "reunited" the two of them five days before his death. That same week the press reported the story of four-year-old Margarita Seeley, whose drug-dealing biological mother forced her to live in a closet and burned her with cigarettes and scalding water after getting the girl back from the loving foster mother who had raised her for the first three years of her life.

Casualties of an Overworked Child Welfare System?

Most of the press commentary about these tragedies portrayed these children as casualties of an overworked, understaffed, and underfunded bureaucracy that "let them slip through the cracks." The subtext: more money will solve the problem, allowing authorities to investigate more reports of abuse. But half of the 1,500 children killed by their parents throughout the country each year are *already* known to the child welfare system. They are victims not of underfunding but of a more fundamental scandal: a "family preservation" policy that the federal government and 30 states, including New York, have carried to absurd and deadly extremes, putting children like Daytwon Bennett and Elisa Izquierdo at grave risk in the name of a skewed notion of civil liberties and parental rights.

It is hard to imagine a more conservative-sounding name for a social policy than family preservation. But in fact, those on the Left who are usually the most hostile to "family values" and parental rights have shaped the policy into its present form and are its most vehement and dogmatic advocates. Family preservation is a classic example of a seemingly sensible and humane liberal reform gone awry because of the ideological single-mindedness of its supporters. The policy now badly hurts those it was meant to help.

Family preservation became a rallying cry in the late 1960s and early 1970s, when a new generation of lawyers and social workers, reacting to the racial and class injustices of the past, charged that culturally biased caseworkers too often removed children from troubled but essentially functional and loving poor families. These reformers wanted to make an attempt to keep such families together—with support services like emergency economic aid and intensive counseling—before removing a child from the home. With help, they argued, these families could weather temporary crises caused by financial or emotional distress—situations in which there was, at worst, short-term neglect or isolated abuse that did not seriously threaten a child. At the time advocates of family preservation never suggested that it would apply to cases in which there was a history or risk of life-threatening abuse because of a parent's drug addiction, mental illness, or sociopathy.

> *"[Children killed by abusive parents] are victims of . . . a 'family preservation' policy that the federal government and 30 states . . . have carried to absurd and deadly extremes."*

By elevating the right of low-income parents to raise their children above the welfare worker's view of the children's best interests, family preservation jibed with the rights revolution then under way. And indeed, it was hard to quarrel with the reformers' basic claim: it is better not to uproot a child from a "troubled but loving" family, even if conditions in the home are less than ideal.

Family Preservation Becomes Law

In the late 1970s legislators began to pass laws to institutionalize family preservation, in language meant to limit the policy to cases where parents did not seriously endanger their children. In order to qualify for federal funding of their foster-care systems under the Adoption Assistance and Child Welfare Act of 1980, states had to make "reasonable efforts" both to keep a family together before taking away a child and to "reunify" the family afterward. Similarly, the New York State Child Welfare Reform Act of 1979 called for "preventive services" when it was "reasonable to believe" that they would enable a child "to remain with or be returned to his family"—that is, when it was reasonable to believe that providing these services would significantly improve the parent's behavior and thus make it safe to leave the child in the home. Subsequent New York legislation required that "reasonable efforts" be made to keep families together "where appropriate."

In the late 1960s, when activists first began pushing for family preservation, one could plausibly claim that "troubled but loving" families were not uncommon, that there were sporadically abusive parents who might change their ways given the proper

> *"Family preservation is a classic example of a seemingly sensible and humane liberal reform gone awry because of the ideological single-mindedness of its supporters."*

support. This key premise of family preservation was far less tenable a decade later, however—at the very moment that legislators began to incorporate the policy into law. By then, the prophecies of observers like Daniel Patrick Moynihan had come true: the problems of the inner-city poor—single-mother families, crime, unemployment, welfare dependency—had grown more and more intractable, only to deepen in the 1980s with the crack cocaine epidemic. Seemingly oblivious to this transformation, child welfare authorities continued to prescribe parenting classes and other "preventive services" that were intended for "troubled but loving" families—despite the fact that today's abusive parents are so often capable of maiming, torturing, and sexually abusing their children.

Perverse Incentives

What led officials routinely to apply family preservation policy to cases involving such parents? Perverse incentives had a lot to do with it. Because states risk the loss of federal funds only for doing too little to preserve families but not for doing too much, the natural inclination of local bureaucrats has been to err on the side of keeping children in dangerous families. The influential Edna McConnell Clark and Annie E. Casey Foundations have reinforced this tendency by devoting millions of dollars to preventive services and promoting them as the first option in even the most extreme cases of abuse. The Clark Foundation, which argues that what others term "'abuse' . . . may reflect a group's cultural norms," has spent some $40 million on family preservation programs over the last decade.

> *"Family preservation has created a sense that all parents—no matter how abusive—have an unchallengeable right to possess their children."*

The dogmatic ideology of these foundations has found a receptive audience among the members of today's social-work establishment, many of whom almost always consider it "reasonable" and "appropriate" to keep families together—and unacceptably "judgmental" to do otherwise. Thus, a caseworker interviewed several years ago in a Clark Foundation-funded Bill Moyers television special deplored the "labeling process" that "categorizes" a crack-addicted single mother as different from a working family unable to afford day care. "If we're a country that believes in the integrity of families," the caseworker obtusely declared, "we should keep all families together."

An Unchallengeable Right?

Because of this unwillingness of contemporary liberalism to make distinctions among what it regards as different cultures and styles of life, many caseworkers now strive to keep even the most sadistic "families" together. In effect, family preservation has created a sense that all parents—no matter how abusive—have an unchallengeable right to possess their children and to receive government services that will make it easier for them to do so. Consider the chilling case of Rufus Chisholm, a Bronx man who killed his five-year-old son by hanging him from a coat rack, rupturing his liver, and crushing his chest— all for taking a piece of cake from the refrigerator. For Chisholm's surviving children, social workers recommended "return to parent" as the "permanency goal." Another example of this mind-set appeared shortly after Elisa Izquierdo's death, when a social worker wrote an op-ed piece for the New York *Daily News* defending preservation services even for "families who may stand by helplessly as one of their own is beaten or murdered by an out-of-control parent."

Unsurprisingly, this philosophy now dominates the legal services establishment as well. The Legal Aid Society and the Legal Services Corporation, which represent many accused parents in abuse and neglect proceedings, have been among the most zealous proponents of family preservation policies. This bias presents a tragic conflict of interest in New York, since the "law guardians" appointed under the Family Court Act to represent the children in these proceedings are almost always Legal Aid attorneys. Meant to provide the court with a third party that stands apart from the parent and the child welfare authorities and speaks only for the child's best interests, Legal Aid law guardians have often proved advocates for family preservation at any cost.

A few months after the authorities had discovered bruises on Daytwon Bennett's face and taken him from his mother for the fourth time, for instance, his Legal Aid law guardian sided with the mother's attorney and successfully argued that he return home, for what would be the last time. The chief of Legal Aid's juvenile rights division told the *New York Times* that "there was no indication that the child was in any danger." But the foster parents who cared for Daytwon for three years say that his Legal Aid law guardian never even met with the child. Legal Aid law guardians for Elisa Izquierdo and Rayvon Evans also supported their return to their biological mothers. Provisions of the child abuse laws meant to recognize the honest efforts of parents to overcome drug addiction—and passed in the days before crack—have further distorted family preservation policy. Prior to 1981, proof of a parent's drug abuse or addiction created a presumption of child neglect under New York State law. But a 1981 amendment bars such a presumption so long as the parent has merely *enrolled* in a rehabilitation program. The parent is not even required to complete the program, much less to have been drug-free for any stretch of time. "This change," as the Children's Aid Society reported in 1996, "made it harder . . . to prove neglect when parents enrolled in a program but did not stop using drugs—a common experience given the low success rate of treatment."

Thus, Elisa Izquierdo's mother, Awilda Lopez, regained custody of her children after undergoing drug rehabilitation, and she kept them despite quickly lapsing back into crack addiction. This loophole in the law also lay at the root of another of the city's grisliest child abuse cases. In August 1996 authorities found the shriveled, emaciated body of four-year-old Nadine Lockwood in the Manhattan apartment of her drug-addicted mother. A victim of deliberate starvation, Nadine weighed a sickening 15 pounds at death. Several years earlier the city had begun a neglect proceeding against her mother, Carla Lockwood, after another one of her five children tested positive for cocaine at birth. But the city closed the case six months later when Lockwood started attending a drug treatment program.

> *"Despite its manifest failures, family preservation has long enjoyed the unquestioning support of legislators."*

A Tragic Joke

The elaborate taxpayer-supported services that go into family preservation add a note of farce to the tragedy. Child welfare agencies furnish the most dysfunctional and abusive "families" with expensive help well beyond the financial reach of most middle-class families. New York State regulations provide for the payment of homemakers and housekeepers to cook, clean, and shop for parents deemed to be in danger of losing their children to foster care. Patrick Murphy, public guardian of Cook County, Illinois, was one of the original architects of family preservation and is now one of its leading critics. As he sees it, such services lavishly reward irresponsible and criminal behavior and are an affront to the many poor people who struggle against tremendous odds to raise their children well.

Family preservation advocates say that this costly assistance reduces the number of foster-care placements and thus saves money in the long run. But Richard Gelles, director of the Family Violence Research Program at the University of Rhode Island and another leading champion of family preservation turned heretic, notes in a recent book that no evidence exists to support this view. More to the point, he argues, it is both offensive and circular to celebrate family preservation because it reduces the number of foster-care placements. By definition, efforts at family preservation entail not placing a child in foster care, at least for a time. The more extreme the adherence to family preservation, the more likely it is that a child will never be placed, regardless of the parent's behavior. By this Orwellian measure, Daytwon Bennett and Elisa Izquierdo were family preservation success stories.

> *"The law must insist that families that grossly abuse their children are not worth preserving."*

As Gelles rightly argues, "the main outcome variable should be child safety." Using this more logical and humane test, researchers at the University of Chicago conducted a two-year study of the Illinois "Family First" program and found that family preservation services made no difference: 25 percent of parents receiving intensive help abused their children again within a year, compared to 22 percent of parents in a control group that received no special assistance.

Some Reforms Are Made

Despite its manifest failures, family preservation has long enjoyed the unquestioning support of legislators. Indeed, in the Family Preservation and Child Protection Reform Act of 1993, Congress allocated $1 billion over five years to support family preservation programs in the states.

But lawmakers have begun to move haltingly in the direction of reform. In 1996 Congress amended the Child Abuse Prevention and Treatment Act (CAPTA) to bar states receiving federal assistance under the law from requiring the reunification of children with parents who have been convicted of the murder, manslaughter, or serious bodily injury of one of their children. While an improvement, the amendment has serious defects. Because it applies only to parents with a previous *criminal conviction* for the most extreme forms of child abuse, it will affect only a handful of even the most egregious cases. Moreover, because it only prohibits states from *requiring* reunification in these extreme cases, states may still *allow* it, and individual judges may still *order* it. Finally, the federal funds at stake under CAPTA amount to far less than those tied to the federal foster-care law's requirement of "reasonable efforts" to keep families together, which Congress left intact.

More encouragingly, in April 1997 the House of Representatives voted to let states bypass family preservation efforts where a child has suffered "aggravated" abuse. Unfortunately, the bill would allow states to define "aggravated" abuse as narrowly as they wished, and judges could still decide to compel family preservation in such cases. What's more, the bill doesn't protect the siblings of such children: states would still have to make "reasonable efforts" to keep them with their demonstrably abusive parents. A bill pending in the Senate, which provides significant new funds for family preservation programs, contains similar loopholes that judges and social workers committed to the old orthodoxy would surely exploit.

Family Preservation Must Be Limited

If we are to avert future tragedies, both Congress and the New York State Legislature must enact legislation that will strictly limit family preservation policy to its original intent. They must amend existing law so that it declares the obvious: that it is *not* "reasonable" or "appropriate" to attempt to preserve or reunify a family when a parent has starved, tortured, sexually abused, severely injured, or abandoned a child. In addition, legislators in Albany must change state law to allow a parent's drug abuse or addiction to be used as evidence of neglect unless the parent has not only completed a rehabilitation program but has also been drug-free for at least a year. State lawmakers should also insist that law guardians have no affiliation with any organization, such as the Legal Aid Society, that routinely represents accused parents in the same proceedings.

The State Legislature should also *require* judges in abuse proceedings to consider a parent's previous abuse of another child—something that current law merely permits. A recent Suffolk County grand jury report documented a case in which a court allowed a 13-month-old boy to remain with his family despite a medical examination showing that he had had 13 broken ribs and two other broken bones *and* despite the fact that his two-year-old brother had died of similar injuries just two months before. Richard Gelles reports that it is not uncommon for judges and caseworkers, imbued with the spirit of family preservation and a twisted notion of due process, to decline even to examine the case files of other horribly abused children in a household for fear of compromising their objectivity.

Termination of Parental Rights

Finally, state and federal legislators should make it far easier in cases of severe abuse to terminate parental rights and free children for adoption, giving seriously abused kids a chance to live in safe, permanent homes. Current law does not allow the termination process even to begin until a child has been in foster care for a year and further "diligent efforts" to reunify the family, on which it places no time limit, have been exhausted. As a result, abused children usually either languish indefinitely in foster care while social workers strive to "rehabilitate" their parents, or bounce back and forth between abusive parents and constantly changing foster homes.

Without these fundamental reforms, staffing increases and bureaucratic tinkering designed to "plug the cracks" in the child welfare system will be useless. If there are to be no more Daytwons or Elisas, the law must insist that families that grossly abuse children are not worth preserving.

The Foster Care System Exposes Children to Abuse

by Danielle Joseph

About the author: *Danielle Joseph is a former foster child and a contributor to* City Limits, *a New York City urban affairs news magazine.*

Imagine yourself a child, at home watching television one afternoon with your brothers and sisters. Suddenly the doorbell rings. Your mother goes to open the door and it's the police. You sense some kind of confusion and as you approach the front of the house, a policeman grabs you, gathers up your other siblings and says, "Get ready, let's go. You are coming with us. You will see your mother soon. You will be gone for only a few days." You are terrified. You try to say "No" and put up some kind of resistance.

And no matter how much your mother protests, she fails to prevent the police from taking you away. You are put in a police car and taken to a strange office where you are surrounded by people who call themselves social workers. After sitting for what seems like forever, you are finally taken to another strange place to live with unfamiliar people.

Weeks pass, and you are left wondering, Why was I taken away? When will I see my mother again? The policeman said it was only for a few days. It's been almost a month. What is going to happen to me?

This scenario comes to life for many New York City children every day. Children are taken from their families and prevented from having any kind of contact with parents and siblings, sometimes for weeks.

The Foster Care Myth

No one would deny there are cases where children must be separated from their parents in order to protect them from serious abuse. But during the last year and a half, since Elisa Izquierdo was killed by her mother, politicians and the press have been demanding that children be quickly pulled away from their parents whenever there's even just a suspicion of abuse or neglect.

But this idea that a child is automatically made safe once he or she is re-

Reprinted from Danielle Joseph, "Fostering Abuse," *City Limits*, August 1, 1997. Reprinted with permission from *City Limits*.

moved from a neglectful or abusive parent is a myth. If only it were that simple. First of all, being taken from your parents is traumatic. And life in foster care can be just as horrible or worse than living with natural parents. Every year, the city's Administration for Children's Services (ACS) investigates more than 1,300 cases of reported abuse or neglect of children in foster homes. Researchers have also found that children in foster care are twice as likely to be abused there as children living at home. Just last month, a little girl was allegedly beaten to death in Brooklyn by members of her foster family.

This is no surprise to me. When I lived in foster homes, my foster parents cared more about their government stipend check than about me. Most of my friends who have been in foster care will agree. Tanya, a friend of mine, says her foster parent told her, "I do not care what you do just as long as I get mine and you do it on the streets." At least when I lived with my natural mother, I knew she took care of me because she cared—not because she was being paid.

My friend Linda Sanchez, now on her own at 17, had it even worse. "My foster mother almost never bought us any food to eat," she says. "Her son and her son-in-law tried to molest me. They even offered me money [for sex]."

Complaints and Denials

It will be a long time before I forgive my agency for allowing one of my foster parents to abuse me and the three foster children I lived with in Bedford-Stuyvesant [a neighborhood in Brooklyn, New York]. Even though my foster mother received a food stipend for us, she spent more on marijuana and cigarettes each week than she spent on food for us in an entire month. And there was psychological abuse. It was not uncommon for her to yell into the intercom, "Bitch, get your ass downstairs. Now!" She was referring to one of us, of course.

I called my social worker at the foster care agency that oversaw my placement and I asked him to investigate this woman. He said I complained too much. I went to his supervisor, who also ignored me. I went so far as to call ACS. The city investigator set up an appointment with my foster parent when I was not around. During the interview she denied all my complaints and the case was dismissed. It does not take a genius to know that an investigator should interview the person making the complaints. But he did not.

> *"Researchers have . . . found that children in foster care are twice as likely to be abused there as children living at home."*

I fear many children who do not need to be separated from their parents will suffer the way my friends and I have. Instead, whenever it's possible, their natural mothers and fathers should be given help to care for them properly. More emphasis should be placed on family preservation. Preventive services should be provided to families in crisis. If the city thinks a child is at risk, it can step in and help the family with counseling, therapy, drug rehabilitation, parenting techniques and whatever else is necessary.

There is one small problem: city statistics show that ACS caseworkers refer 40 percent fewer families to preventive services today than they did five years ago. Parents nowadays are more likely than ever before to lose their children to foster care. This is a direct result of the ignorant attitudes of reporters, editorial writers and politicians. Foster care has become a political football game of kicking around children and their families. "Remove children at the first sign of abuse," the tabloids scream. "Deranged mothers are destroying their children's lives."

But I know the abuse my friends and I witnessed first-hand in foster care. Rescuing a child is much more complicated than just taking her away from her mother.

Parental Cohabitation Exposes Children to a Greater Risk of Abuse

by John A. Barnes

About the author: *John A. Barnes is an editorial writer for the* New York Post.

On the night of February 23, 1997, Dallas paramedics were summoned to the apartment that Dionne Pickens shared with her son, 2-year-old Devonta, her daughter, 8-year-old Deandrea, and her boyfriend of two months, 25-year-old Abdullah Youself Blackmon. Little Devonta Pickens was unconscious. Blackmon claimed the boy had fallen into a wooden bed railing.

A quick examination showed that couldn't possibly be true. The boy's 30-pound body was covered with welts, including no fewer than five sites of blunt-force trauma to the head. Medical examiners said later the injuries were comparable to what a person would receive in a severe car wreck. Devonta never regained consciousness and soon died.

At his trial, Blackmon admitted hitting the boy but not intending to kill him. He also admitted beating Deandrea earlier in the evening. What had prompted his homicidal rage against the 2-year-old? The latter, he said, had wet his bed.

While all this was going on, the children's mother was in the next room. At some point, Dionne Pickens testified, she no longer heard Devonta crying but continued to hear the belt striking the child.

The jury wasn't buying the idea that Devonta Pickens's death was an accident. Blackmon was convicted on October 2, 1998, and sentenced to life in prison, of which he must serve at least 40 years before becoming eligible for parole.

Just two days after Blackmon's conviction, 3-year-old Ashley Smithson of Miami was disconnected from the life-support machines that had been keeping her alive for a month after her head was slammed into a wall by Juvon D. Pickett, the 18-year-old boyfriend of Ashley's mother, Pecynthia Bradley. During her short life, the little girl had already been hospitalized twice after punishment at Pickett's hands. Her mother, too, stood by and watched while her daughter was being killed.

In Brooklyn in December 1997, Luis Santiago was convicted of manslaughter for his role in the death of Justina Morales. The tot's mother, Denise Solero, testified that she held the child's hands steady while Santiago strangled the life out of her and helped to dispose of the body afterwards. "Mommy, make me pretty," were Justina's last words.

Open virtually any big-city newspaper and you will find a depressingly large number of such stories. A young child, living with his mother in a cramped apartment, is beaten to within an inch of his life—or, as in the cases cited above, meets death—at the hands of Mom's boyfriend/ex-husband/live-in, often while Mom looks on.

What is remarkable about such cases, however, is that they draw almost no systematic attention (much less condemnation) from anyone in a position of authority. In a country that obsesses over the effect of secondhand smoke on its children, that worries incessantly about "at-risk" youngsters, and whose chief executive is wont to use children's welfare as a justification for virtually any policy prescription of the moment, this is a significant oversight.

Systematic studies of the problem are indeed few and far between. "We don't have anything specifically on that," said a spokesman for the U.S. Department of Justice's Office of Justice Programs, though two of its divisions, the Bureau of Justice Statistics

> *"The statistical danger to a child is vastly increased by the presence of an unrelated man in the household."*

and the National Institute of Justice, do nothing but collect statistics on crime-related problems.

The few studies that have been done, however, confirm what common sense already dictates: The statistical danger to a child is vastly increased by the presence of an unrelated man in the household.

A March 1996 study by the Bureau of Justice Statistics contains some interesting findings that indicate just how widespread the problem may be. In a nationally representative survey of state prisoners jailed for assaults against or murders of children, fully one-half of respondents reported the victim was a friend, acquaintance, or relative other than offspring. (All but 3 percent of those who committed violent crimes against children were men.) A close relationship between victim and victimizer is also suggested by the fact that three-quarters of all the crimes occurred in either the perpetrator's home or the victim's.

A 1994 paper published in the *Journal of Comparative Family Studies* looked at 32,000 documented cases of child abuse. Of the victims, only 28 percent lived with both biological parents (far fewer than the 68 percent of all children who live with both parents); 44 percent lived with their mother only (as do 25 percent of all children); and 18 percent lived with their mother and an unrelated adult (double the 9 percent of all children who live with their mother and an un-related adult).

These findings mirror a 1993 British study by the Family Education Trust, which meticulously explored the relationship between family structure and child abuse. Using data on documented cases of abuse in Britain between 1982 and 1988, the report found a high correlation between child abuse and the marital status of the parents.

Specifically, the British study found that the incidence of abuse was an astounding 33 times higher in homes where the mother was cohabiting with an unrelated boyfriend than in stable nuclear families. Even when the boyfriend was the children's biological father, the chances of abuse were twice as high.

These findings are consonant with those published a year earlier by Leslie Margolin of the University of Iowa in the journal *Child Abuse and Neglect*. Professor Margolin found that boyfriends were 27 times more likely than natural parents to abuse a child. The next-riskiest group, siblings, were only twice as likely as parents to abuse a child.

More recently, a report by Dr. Michael Stiffman presented at the American Academy of Pediatrics, in October 1998, studied the 175 Missouri children under the age of 5 who were murdered between 1992 and 1994. It found that the risk of a child's dying at the hands of an adult living in the child's own household was eight times higher if the adult was biologically unrelated.

The Connection Between Child Abuse and Cohabitation

The Heritage Foundation's Patrick Fagan discovered that the number of child-abuse cases appeared to rise in the 1980s along with the general societal acceptance of cohabitation before, or instead of, marriage. That runs counter to the radical-feminist view, which holds that marriage is an oppressive male institution of which violence is an integral feature. If that were true, then child abuse and domestic violence should have decreased along with the rise in cohabitation.

Heritage also found that in the case of very poor children (those in households earning less than $15,000 per year), 75 percent lived in a household where the biological father was absent. And 50 percent of adults with less than a high-school education lived in cohabitation arrangements. "This mix—poverty, lack of education, children, and cohabitation—is an incubator for violence," Fagan says.

Why, then, do we ignore the problem? Fagan has a theory: "It is extremely politically incorrect to suggest that living together might not be the best living arrangement."

"It is the great unmentionable," says David Blankenhorn, president of the New York-based Institute for American Values and the author of *Fatherless America*. "To bring up the boyfriend problem seems too much like you're passing judgment on the sexual behavior of single mothers."

Indeed, you will search in vain the Web sites of the major organizations supposedly dedicated to combating child abuse for any mention of the boyfriend problem. The National Clearinghouse on Child Abuse and Neglect, for example, lists the following as "primary" means of preventing child abuse: (1) "Public service announcements . . . encouraging parents to use non-violent forms of discipline." (2) "Parent education programs and groups teaching parents age-appropriate expectations." (3) "Public awareness campaigns informing citizens how and where to report suspected child abuse and neglect."

While acknowledging that abuse by boyfriends is a problem, Joy Byers, then-communications director of the National Committee to Prevent Child Abuse, became defensive when pressed as to why her organization doesn't highlight it. "Are you saying that single parents don't have the right to date or have adult friends in the house?" she asked.

In fact, culture-shaping vehicles such as movies and television shows as well as public-service announcements are more likely to imply or state that a child's father or stepfather (almost invariably portrayed as a respectable suburbanite) represents the greatest threat to the child. Remember Ted Danson's portrayal of such a father in the made-for-TV movie *Something About Amelia*? Or the husband in Farrah Fawcett's *The Burning Bed*?

It's easy to see why irresponsible sexual behavior militates against responsible parenthood. "The boyfriend's interest is in the child's mother," says a New York Police Department detective who specializes in domestic-violence cases and who asks not to be identified. "The kids' interest, of course, is also in their mother. So it sets up an almost automatic tug-of-war-type contest almost from the get-go. The boyfriend has no emotional or biological interest in the kids, so they are frequently seen as being 'in the way.'"

The boyfriend's uncertain status in the household makes the potential for explosion exceptionally high when he attempts to discipline the children.

"If mothers' boyfriends believe they lack legitimate authority in their partner's family, they may anticipate that other family members will not obey or respect them," says Professor Margolin. "This leaves them defensive, looking for and reacting to affronts that are not there." As a consequence, boyfriends may be quicker to use violence against the children than natural fathers would be and may use it with less restraint when they do.

> *"The incidence of abuse was an astounding 33 times higher in homes where the mother was cohabiting with an unrelated boyfriend than in stable nuclear families."*

The boyfriend problem is partly a product, too, of the devaluation of fatherhood since the sexual revolution. While shelves of books have been written about the impact of the feminist movement on women, few have been written about its impact on men.

One effect, it seems, has been to encourage a sense that fathers are expendable. Parenting has come to be identified more than ever with "maternal" qualities—emotional nurturing, the easy expression of affection, and discomfort with discipline. Government seems to take a crudely materialistic view of fathers—slighting divorced fathers when it comes to enforcing visitation rights, for example, but noticing them as soon as they become "deadbeats."

Well, fathers are not simply sperm banks, or ATM machines, or pinch-hitters for when Mommy gets tired. It is their duty to keep their children safe from the harm others might inflict on them. Sadly, children's behavior is often not lovable, except by those with a primal interest in seeing their offspring grow and flourish. In other words, one of the main purposes of the nuclear family is to protect children from men who are not their fathers.

Child abuse is as old as the family itself, and it is true that in absolute numbers, far more children are abused by their parents than by anyone else. But the boyfriend problem is something new. It grows directly out of the looser social structure that has grown up in America since the 1960s. And since it is relatively recent, we have a fighting chance of being able to do something about it.

The social sanction given to cohabitation is of recent vintage. It can be reversed. But to build a consensus for restigmatizing cohabitation, and thus to start reversing the boyfriend problem, we need more information. Government agencies that are on the front lines, dealing with abused children daily, should begin systematically gathering information on family structure. This would be a fairly simple and cheap way of establishing empirically the dangers of what used to be called "living in sin."

Once this information is gathered, it will be possible to act on it. It wasn't long ago that a woman sharing living quarters with an unmarried man was considered prima facie an unfit mother. Social-service agencies can begin flagging kids living in such circumstances for special attention and, where necessary, even removing more children from such situations.

And how about a few public-service announcements simply to raise public awareness of the dangers of sharing living quarters with a man who refuses to make a commitment to marriage?

Meanwhile, there is at least one encouraging sign that the boyfriend problem is coming out of the closet. An off-Broadway play, "You Shouldn't Have Told," by Anne Thompson-Scretching, has been packing them in at various New York venues since January 1997. Thompson-Scretching herself is the product of a boyfriend-problem household, and she has written a raw and emotionally charged night of theater that explores the horrific consequences of a mother's allowing her no-good boyfriend to move in with her and her family.

"For a long, long time, this was a taboo subject, especially in the black community," the playwright says. Her willingness to admit the gravity of the problem sets a good example for the rest of us.

Poverty Causes Child Abuse

by Leroy H. Pelton

About the author: *Leroy H. Pelton is a professor in the School of Social Work at Salem State College in Salem, Massachusetts. He is the author of* For Reasons of Poverty: A Critical Analysis of the Public Child Welfare System in the United States, *from which this viewpoint is excerpted.*

There is by now overwhelming evidence of a strong relationship between poverty and child abuse and neglect. The great majority of families to whom child abuse and neglect have been attributed live in poverty or near-poverty circumstances. This finding has been obtained across a range of methodologies and definitions. Moreover, poverty is the single most prevalent characteristic of these families, who tend to be the *poorest* of the poor.

Every national survey of officially reported child neglect and abuse incidents has indicated that the preponderance of the reports have involved families from the lowest socioeconomic levels. In the earliest of these studies, a nationwide survey of child-abuse reports made to central registries, [David G.] Gil found that nearly 60 percent of the families involved in the abuse incidents had been on welfare during or prior to the study year of 1967, and 37.2 percent of the abusive families had been receiving public assistance at the time of the incident.

Data collected by The American Humane Association (AHA), through its annual national study of official child abuse and neglect reporting, have showed that for the year 1976, for example, 42 percent of the families in validated reports were receiving public assistance. The median family income was $5,051 (which is at the 1976 poverty level for a family of four), compared with about $13,900 for all American families in 1976. About two-thirds of the families in validated reports had incomes under $7,000, and only 9 percent of the families had incomes of $13,000 or more. For reports of neglect only, the median income was slightly lower ($4,250) than for abuse only ($6,882).

These same trends have continued year after year in a rather stable fashion.

The AHA data for the year 1977 indicated that 47.1 percent of the involved families in substantiated reports had incomes of less than $5,000 per year, while only 5.9 percent had incomes of at least $16,000, which was the median family income for all U.S. families in 1977. Moreover, 43.7 percent of the families were receiving public assistance. The AHA data for the year 1981 showed 43 percent of the reported families were receiving public assistance, compared with 11 percent of all U.S. families. In 1986, 48.9 percent of the reported families were receiving public assistance, compared with 12 percent of all U.S. families.

This poverty relationship is not just a recent phenomenon, of course. In a study of cases known to the Massachusetts Society for the Prevention of Cruelty to Children (SPCC) and other private social service agencies in the Boston area from 1880 to 1960, Gordon documented that the most pronounced characteristic of the clients in family violence cases was their poverty.

The Socioeconomic Pattern of Abuse Has Not Changed

While it is true, as has often been argued, that poor people are more susceptible to public scrutiny and are thus more likely than others to be *reported* for abuse or neglect, it has been shown that the relationship between poverty and child abuse and neglect is not just an anomaly of reporting systems. First, while greater public awareness and new reporting laws led to a significant increase in official reporting over the years, the socioeconomic pattern of these reports has not changed appreciably. We might have expected an expanded and more vigilant public watch to produce an increased proportion of reports from above the lower class, but this has not happened.

Second, the "public scrutiny" argument cannot explain the evidence that child abuse and neglect are related to *degrees* of poverty, even *within* that same lower class which is acknowledgedly more open to public scrutiny. In the Isabel Wolock and Bernard Horowitz study, Aid to Families with Dependent Children (AFDC) families involved in child abuse and neglect cases were found to be living in more crowded and dilapidated households, to have been more likely to have gone hungry, and in general, to be existing at a lower material level of living than the other AFDC families studied.

> *"The great majority of families to whom child abuse and neglect have been attributed live in poverty or near-poverty circumstances."*

Third, the "public scrutiny" argument cannot explain why the severest injuries have occurred within the poorest families, even among the reported cases. Moreover, it cannot explain why child homicide studies have indicated that child abuse and neglect fatalities, which are certainly less easy to hide from public scrutiny than milder abuse and neglect incidents, have predominantly occurred in poor families.

Finally, evidence of a more direct nature was collected in the Westat National

Incidence Study, which was designed to go beyond the officially reported cases of child abuse and neglect known to child protective service agencies. It did so by additionally gathering information on abuse and neglect incidents directly from other agencies, such as police and public health departments, and from professionals in hospitals, mental health facilities, other social service agencies, and public schools. The study found that the annual income of the families of 43 percent of the victims was under $7,000, compared with an estimated 17 percent of all U. S. children who lived in families with

> *"It has been shown that the relationship between poverty and child abuse and neglect is not just an anomaly of reporting systems."*

income that low. Fully 82 percent of the victims were from families with incomes below $15,000, in comparison with 45 percent of all U.S. children. Only 6 percent of the victims were from families with incomes of $25,000 or more. The relationship between low income and child maltreatment was less pronounced for abuse than for neglect, but still strong. The study concluded that the strong relationship between poverty and child abuse and neglect is not largely explainable in terms of reporting biases because the relationship "is almost as strong for unreported cases as for those which are reported to Child Protective Services." A follow-up to the National Incidence Study showed that, in the year 1986, the relationship between low income and overall maltreatment continued to be strong. In fact, in only 6 percent of the cases was the family income $30,000 or more.

The Problems of Poverty

In light of these facts, the conclusion that problems of poverty might be partial determinants of child abuse and neglect is inescapable. Indeed, it has been theorized that the problems of poverty may generate stressful experiences that become precipitating factors in child abuse and neglect. Such factors as unemployment, dilapidated and overcrowded housing, and insufficient money, food, recreation, or hope can provide the stressful context for abusive as well as neglectful behavior. Such stresses can provoke the anger that may lead to abuse, as well as the despair that may lead to neglect when, for example, a single parent attempts to raise a large family in cramped and unsafe living quarters with no help and little money.

Certainly, parents are responsible for their own behavior, regardless of whether we interpret it in terms of stress or other factors. Yet in most cases, there is multiple causation of the risk of harm to children, and a sole fixation on the parents themselves, which has indeed been fostered by the framing of child welfare problems in terms of "abuse and neglect" and by the psychodynamic medical model, would be overly simplistic.

Impoverished families tend to live, though not by choice, in neighborhoods with the highest crime rates, in apartments that are not secure, and in homes made dangerous by lack of heating, poor wiring and exposed lead paint, to name only a few of the health and safety hazards associated with poverty. These conditions, which are among the very same ones that may cause indirect danger to children by generating stressful experiences for the parents, also cause direct danger for which it is all too easy to implicate the parents for not preventing. Moreover, in the presence of these conditions, poor people have very little leeway for lapses in responsibility.

In addition, a low-income mother with many children cannot easily obtain or pay for a babysitter every time she wants or needs to leave the house. If she leaves her children alone, she is gambling with their safety; if she stays with them, she may be unable to do her shopping in order to provide food and other necessities. Thus, she may be caught up in a difficult situation that has less to do with her adequacy and responsibility as a parent than with the hard circumstances of her life.

The Inability to Cope with Poverty

It is true that only a small proportion of poor people are even alleged to abuse or neglect their children. The most reasonable conclusion that can be drawn from the nature of the relationship between poverty and child abuse and neglect is that poverty is often a contributing factor, a partial determinant that often provides the context for abuse and neglect, and that there must be other *mediating* factors between poverty and these resultants. These mediators might well include parent-centered, personal, and psychological problems and characteristics, although just what characteristics these might be remains unclear. However, the doubts cast upon the validity of the personality characteristics that have been implied in the literature, together with the strong relationship found between poverty and child abuse and neglect, lead one to suspect that if any personal traits are prevalent among parents in abuse and neglect cases, they might be ones that have more to do with the ability or inability to cope with poverty and its stresses than anything else. Indeed, other factors frequently associated with child protection cases include health problems, social isolation, family discord, and alcohol or drug dependence.

> *"The problems of poverty may generate stressful experiences that become precipitating factors in child abuse and neglect."*

Regardless of how we or society decide to apportion blame or responsibility, one thing is clear: Many of the families in child abuse and neglect cases lack resources and need help. Yet in a large proportion of the cases reported to public child welfare agencies, the result has not been help to the family as a whole, but child removal.

Indeed, the proponents of the myth of classlessness, by invoking the public scrutiny argument in attempting to deny the relationship of child abuse and neglect and poverty, were obscuring the significance of the fact of the strong relationship between *reported* alleged abuse and neglect and poverty. The significance is that the families being reported to child protection agencies in the 1970s were, just as they had always been throughout this century and before, predominantly from among the poorest families in our society, and that therefore the children being removed into foster care were the same ones as

> *"Many of the families in child abuse and neglect cases lack resources and need help."*

they had always been in this respect. The only difference was that in the 1960s and 1970s . . . due to a child abuse crusade backed by unprecedented funding, more poor families than ever before were being reported to and investigated by child protection agencies, and more such children than ever before were being removed. . . .

Poverty and Sexual Abuse

Poverty is just as much associated with sexual abuse as with other forms of child maltreatment. The first Westat National Incidence Study . . . found the relationship between low income and sexual abuse to be just as strong as that between low income and overall child abuse and neglect, in that 80 percent of the families of sexual abuse victims had annual incomes under $15,000, and only 2 percent had incomes of $25,000 or more. The follow-up National Incidence Study, also mentioned above, showed that in 1986, the low-income relationship continued to be strong for sexual abuse. The incidence of sexual abuse was four to five times higher among children from families whose income was less than $15,000 than those from families whose income was $15,000 or more.

These studies included incidents not involving genital contact in their definitions of sexual abuse, but only when there was evidence that such noncontact experiences might have caused at least some physical or emotional trauma to the. child. Other studies, employing broader definitions and a variety of methodologies, have not always found this low-income relationship. Since the preponderance of the incidents counted in the National Incidence studies did involve genital contact, it is clear that the low-income relationship holds for these more severe forms of sexual abuse, and it is likely that the relationship between low income and sexual abuse has been "washed out" in some studies through the inclusion of higher proportions of incidents involving noncontact and questionable forms of sexual abuse. Any adequate perspectives on sexual abuse will have to take the socioeconomic facts into account.

To sum up, the factors responsible for the explosion in the foster care placement rates during the 1960s and 1970s were: (1) the psychodynamic medical model, which encouraged us to blame the individual results of the conditions of poverty on poor people and to look for personal defects in them; (2) the myth of classlessness, which encouraged the inclination to label impoverished parents as psychologically defective and to ignore the socioeconomic factors involved; (3) the numbers illusion, which encouraged the public's apparent inclination to blame parents and to believe that there were many cruel parents out there deliberately battering their children; (4) the public awareness campaigns and reporting laws, which were both cause and effect of the child abuse crusade; and (5) the social service funding that was misguidedly funneled into investigation and foster care rather than into the provision of concrete services.

A Parental History of Abuse Is a Major Risk Factor in Child Abuse

by Byron Egeland

About the author: *Byron Egeland is the Irving B. Harris professor of child development at the University of Minnesota. He is a fellow in the American Psychological Association and the American Psychological Society and has served on a number of national committees in the area of child abuse.*

Over the more than 30 years since C. Henry Kempe, Frederic N. Silverman, Brandt F. Steele, William Droegemueller, and Henry K. Silver's description of the "battered child syndrome," a tremendous amount has been written about the causes of child maltreatment. Much of the early writing reported that abusing parents were themselves abused, which led to the belief in the transmission of abuse or a cycle of abuse across generations. This notion of the intergenerational transmission of abuse was one of the earliest and most widely accepted theories of abuse. J.J. Spinetta and D. Rigler note that "one of the basic factors in the etiology of child abuse draws unanimity: abusing parents were themselves abused or neglected physically or emotionally as children." It continues to be accepted as a significant factor in the etiology of abuse. Cathy Spatz Widom notes that it currently is the "premier" hypothesis in the field of abuse and neglect. The popularity and longevity of the intergenerational hypothesis is the result of many factors, including the fact that it makes intuitive sense and thus has popular appeal.

Support for the notion that child maltreatment is transmitted across generations has also come from the general belief in the cycle of violence—violence begets violence. There is considerable evidence from research on delinquent behavior; homicides; aggressive, violent behavior in young children; and family violence to support the notion of a cycle of violence. In the area of family violence, Maria Roy found that 80% of abusive husbands had been abused as children or had witnessed their fathers abusing their mothers. Murray Straus, Richard Gelles, and Suzanne Steinmetz found that men and women who grew up in violent homes were far more likely to abuse their spouses than were men and women who grew up in nonviolent homes. Straus et al. conclude that each generation learns to be violent by participating in a violent family. In general, there is considerable evidence to support the notion that violence breeds violence.

Despite the popular belief in the cycle of violence, an increasing number of professionals are raising questions about the intergenerational hypothesis. In the area of child abuse, Joan Kaufman and Edward Zigler argue that the rate of transmission across generations is overstated, at least in the popular press. In addition, they warn that popularizing the intergenerational hypothesis will have negative consequences and unnecessarily raise fears in prospective parents who have histories of having been abused. . . .

Empirical Support for the Intergenerational Hypothesis

The bulk of the empirical evidence in support of the intergenerational hypothesis in the area of child maltreatment has come from retrospective studies. This approach involves looking backward in time as abusing parents are studied after they have been identified as having abused their own children. Investigators using the retrospective approach, with or without comparison groups of nonabusive parents, usually find that a large majority of abusing parents were abused as children. For example, B.J. Steele and C.B. Pollock found that all 60 abusing parents in their study were abused as children. They conclude that a basic factor in the "genesis" of child abuse is the treatment the parents received during their childhood.

One reason Kaufman and Zigler claim that the case for the intergenerational hypothesis is overstated is that the findings from retrospective research overestimate the rate of transmission of abuse across generations. The problem with the retrospective approach is that it cannot determine what proportion of adults who were maltreated as children are providing adequate care for their own children. The retrospective approach provides information about the percentage of abusers who were abused as children, but it does not provide information about the caregiving behavior of all individuals who were abused. It appears that the majority of abusing parents were themselves abused, but it may also be the case that the majority

> *"One of the basic factors in the etiology of child abuse draws unanimity: abusing parents were themselves abused or neglected physically or emotionally as children."*

of parents who were abused as children are providing adequate care. Looking backward, the rate of abuse across generations is high; looking forward, using a prospective approach, the rate is likely to be lower. Unfortunately, there has never been a true prospective study, where a group of abused children were followed into adulthood and the quality of their parenting assessed. Following a group of abused children into adulthood would no doubt uncover a rate of abuse across generations that would be lower than the 100% rate found by Steele and others who have used retrospective data. It is important that investigators be cautious in interpreting the findings of retrospective studies.

An Underestimation of Abuse

As noted above, Kaufman and Zigler argue that the retrospective approach leads to an overestimate of the rate of transmission. Perhaps this is true, but there may also be reasons the retrospective approach may result in an *under-estimate* of the rate of transmission. It is possible that interviewing parents about their own childhoods may result in an underestimate of the actual number who were abused. Charles Zeanah and P.D. Zeanah point out that some parents who were abused as children believe that physical punishment and neglect are normal, or at least acceptable. If asked if they were abused as children, some abused adults would say no because they believe that the harsh treatment they received from their parents is acceptable. An indeterminable number of parents whose treatment as children could be considered abuse do not perceive themselves as having been abused.

> *"There is considerable evidence to support the notion that violence breeds violence."*

A second reason for underreports of maltreatment during childhood is that some parents describe their own parents and childhood experiences in idealized fashion. Mary Biggar Main and R. Goldwyn and others have found that some abused parents describe their parents in global and positive terms and, when encouraged to give examples of the care they received as children, are unable to describe specific situations. These parents have idealized their childhood experiences. Main and Goldwyn describe the process of idealization as part of a defensive strategy that individuals develop to cope with the trauma of abuse. Idealization is one form of dissociation, which is a mechanism sometimes used by individuals to cope with traumatic experiences. Other dissociative symptoms include an inability to recall traumatic experiences, the extreme forms of which are psychogenic amnesia, fugue states, and multiple personality disorder. Thus idealization and other factors that cause underreporting of a history of having been abused as a child may lead to underestimates of the rate of transmission.

Investigations of Maltreatment Across Generations

It is difficult to judge the accuracy of Kaufman and Zigler's estimated rate of transmission of abuse of 30%, because it is based on only three quasi-prospective investigations. In reviewing these investigations, one could find reasons to support an argument for a higher rate.

78

Two of the three prospective studies found an 18% rate of transmission of abuse across generations. My colleagues and I found a rate of 40% using a broader definition of *maltreatment* that included parents who were psychologically unavailable. There are a number of reasons the 18% rate found by Straus and R.S. Hunter et al. is an underestimate. Straus's early study, which is basically a retrospective study, consisted of a large national sample of two-parent families with children between the ages of 3 and 17. His rate of 18% is likely an underestimate because the sample was limited to two-parent families with children over age 3. In fact, much child abuse takes place in single-parent families, and much abuse occurs prior to age 3. In addition, parents were identified as having histories of abuse if they indicated that they were physically punished during adolescence. Adolescence is a period when physical punishment is *least* likely to occur. The majority of parents who were abused as children were probably omitted from the "history of punishment" category. . . .

> **"A large majority of abusing parents were abused as children."**

Based on findings from the Mother-Child Project, a longitudinal study of high-risk parents and their children, I found a rate of maltreatment across generations of 40%, which is slightly higher than the 30% estimated by Kaufman and Zigler. My data are based on a sample of 267 first-time pregnant women who were enrolled in their last trimester of pregnancy and who have been followed over the past 16 years. The mothers were considered at risk for caregiving problems because of their low socioeconomic status (SES), youthfulness, unmarried status, and lack of support.

Within this high-risk sample, 44 cases of maltreatment were identified, which included physical abuse, neglect, hostile/rejecting, and psychologically unavailable patterns of caretaking. Overlap among these four categories of maltreatment was considerable; for example, 15 of the 19 children who experienced hostile/rejecting mothers were also physically abused. In addition, there was an "other" problem group that consisted of mothers who were not the primary caretakers of their children. One mother in this group traveled with a circus and saw very little of her child, and others had basically abandoned their children for other reasons.

Mothers in all maltreatment groups were identified on the basis of information obtained from mother interviews, home visits, and observations of mother and child in home and laboratory situations. These data were obtained at regular intervals, starting at birth and continuing through preschool. The maltreatment groups were formed based on data collected through the preschool period. A total of 18 assessments occurred between the neonatal period and 48 months of age.

Independent of the identification of mothers who were maltreating their children, we determined the quality of care the mothers received when they were children. At the time of the 48- and 54-month assessments, each mother was asked a series of questions about her childhood and family of origin, including whether or not she was reared by a relative or placed in a foster home. She was asked about how she was disciplined and whether or not she was beaten or physically abused, sexually molested, or neglected. On the basis of the responses, 47 mothers were identified as having been maltreated as children. Women who were not abused were further divided into those who were emotionally supported as children (35 women) and the remainder of the sample. Emotionally supportive families were described as loving, concerned, and encouraging.

Of the 47 mothers who were abused as children, 16 (34%) were currently maltreating their children and 3 (6%) were in the other problems group, resulting in a 40% rate of maltreatment across generations. Within this group of 47 mothers who were abused as children, 13 mothers reported having been sexually abused as children by a family member. Of these, 6 (46%) maltreated their children, and 2 were having other problems (15%). Altogether, 61% of the mothers who reported having been sexually abused as children were maltreating their children.

> *"If asked if they were abused as children, some abused adults would say no because they believe that the harsh treatment they received from their parents is acceptable."*

From the total sample of 47 mothers who were abused as children, a sizable proportion (40%) were maltreating their children; however, it is important to note that the majority of the abused parents provided adequate care. A history of abuse is a major risk factor for abusing, but it is not a guarantee that abuse will occur in the next generation. There are many additional risk factors that need to be considered in order to understand the causes and varied "courses" of child maltreatment. . . .

In summary, my colleagues and I have found the rate of transmission of abuse to be 40%, which I believe to be a conservative estimate. Regardless of whether the rate of transmission is 30%, as estimated by Kaufman and Zigler, or higher, as we and others have found, the association is substantial and should not be ignored by researchers or practitioners in the field. A transmission rate of 40% is at least 13 times greater than the highest national estimate of the rate of child abuse.

Breaking the Cycle of Abuse

Much of our research having to do with the transmission of abuse across generations has focused on the question, Why do some abused individuals break the cycle of abuse? To answer this question, my colleagues and I compared mothers who were abused in childhood and who abused their children (continuity group) to mothers who were abused but provided adequate care for their own children (exception group). I will summarize these findings, which have been reported in detail elsewhere.

One set of variables that distinguished mothers who broke the cycle of abuse from those in the continuity group had to do with the availability of emotionally supportive individuals. Mothers who broke the cycle were, as children, more likely to have had foster parents or relatives who provided them with emotional support. Even though a woman was abused as a child, there was someone there for nurturance and support. Another relationship variable distinguishing the two groups was the mother's relationship with a husband/boyfriend. Most of the mothers who broke the cycle were in intact, stable, and satisfying relationships. One mother who gave birth at age 18 and who continues to live with the father of the child described the father as supportive and accepting. She described how she has come to trust him and how, within this trusting relationship, she has changed her expectations regarding close relationships. At times, she reported, she becomes frustrated and upset in disciplining her child, but she is able to seek help and support from her mate.

> *"A history of abuse is a major risk factor for abusing, but it is not a guarantee that abuse will occur in the next generation."*

Another relationship variable that distinguished the continuity and exception groups was involvement in psychotherapy as an adolescent or young adult. A number of mothers who broke the cycle of abuse were in long-term, intensive psychotherapy. One of our mothers who was most severely abused as a child was removed from her mother at age 11 and placed in a succession of foster homes. In the third foster home, she took pills to get high, which was interpreted as a suicide attempt. Because there were limited treatment options in the rural area where she lived, she was sent to a hospital that treated chemically dependent adults. During her two-year stay in the hospital she received a great deal of emotional support from other patients, along with intensive psychotherapy. Through therapy and support, the mother became aware of her child-rearing history and how it might affect the child care she provided her children.

This mother described her abusive experiences in an integrated and coherent fashion. The experiences were reported with much emotion, and she provided specific examples to support her view of her parents. This integration of the abusive experience into her view of herself was typical of mothers who broke the cycle of abuse. Mothers who broke the cycle of abuse seemed to be aware of how their early experiences affected their expectations regarding relationships. They were aware of the effects of their childhood histories of abuse on their current feelings about themselves and significant others, particularly their children. In general, they were more insightful in their understanding of themselves and seemed to have better understanding of their relationships with their children than did mothers who did not break the cycle.

Splitting Off

Mothers who did not break the cycle of abuse seemed to dissociate or "split off" the abusive experience rather than integrating it into a view of themselves. Many of these mothers idealized their pasts, unrealistically describing their parents and childhood experiences as all good. Such descriptions were basically fantasy; they were incongruent with actual experiences. One of the mothers went on at length about the great time she had as a child with her father. She described him as a wonderful man, but she could not give any specific examples of childhood activities with her father. We later learned that he had a serious drinking problem and that he abandoned the family when she was 2 years old. Other mothers seemed "detached" from their parents and childhoods. They had difficulty recalling childhood experiences and avoided talking about their parents. It was common for these mothers to make comments such as "I am having trouble remembering" or "My mind just goes blank when I try to remember my childhood." They talked about their histories of abuse in a vague, disconnected fashion, as if the abuse never really happened to them. Typically, they displayed little emotion when describing their abusive experiences.

Even though these findings are very tentative, it appears that some mothers who were abused as children coped with the traumatic experience by "splitting off" or dissociating. They repeated the abusive pattern in their relationships with their children because they did not see the connection between their current behaviors and their pasts. Because they dissociated from their own experiences, they did not associate the pain they felt as children with the pain they inflicted on their own children. The abusive experiences were not memories on which they could reflect; instead, the early experiences were repeatedly acted out.

John Briere found that women who have been sexually abused often dissociate or "split off" this traumatic experience. F.W. Putnam, J.J. Guroff, E.K. Silberman, L. Barban, and R.M. Post, in a study of multiple personality disorder, an extreme form of dissociation, found a high incidence of severe physical and sexual abuse in their sample. Despite very little empirical knowledge about dissociation as a coping strategy for dealing with trau-

> *"[Abused parents] repeated the abusive pattern . . . because they did not see the connection between their current behaviors and their pasts."*

matic experience, and even less about the role it may play in explaining the intergenerational transmission of abuse, there are a number of interesting hypotheses that need to be investigated.

There are other mechanisms that may help us understand the processes by which maltreatment is transmitted across generations. We have hypothesized that attachment theory may "explain the cycle of abuse." [John] Bowlby notes that the early caregiver-infant attachment relationship is a prototype of later relationships. During the course of the first year of life, infants form strong emotional relationships with their primary caregivers. This attachment is necessary for the survival of the infant. As part of this relationship, the infant develops representational models or, to use Bowlby's term, inner working models of self and significant others. At an early age, the child constructs a cognitive model that best fits the reality experienced. As the child grows older, new relationships are assimilated into existing models as long as the new experiences don't deviate too greatly from the existing models. These models are maintained largely outside of awareness, and they provide the child with a set of expectations about self and relationships that in turn influence the child's behavior in relationships. Zeanah and T.F. Anders have noted that inner working models compel an individual to re-create experiences congruent with his or her relationship history. Sroufe observed children in preschool who were classified as secure or anxiously attached in infancy and found support for this notion that the children re-created relationships with their teachers that were consistent with their earlier relationships with their primary caregivers.

Expectations of Rejection and Hostility

A child who has a history of abuse expects others to be rejecting, hostile, and unavailable. A child who has been neglected (physically, emotionally, or both) expects others to be unresponsive, unavailable, and not willing to meet his or her needs. Maltreated children bring these expectations to relationships, and they respond to others in a fashion consistent with their expectations.

Zeanah and Zeanah make the argument that early patterns of relating and the development of inner working models have more far-reaching consequences than do specific traumatic events. The child's subjective view of the abusive experience forms the basis of the inner working model. It is the "meaning context" of the maltreating behavior that forms the theme of what is internalized and becomes a "working model." The violence per se is not passed on from one generation to the next; rather, the ongoing theme of the caregiving relationship is transmitted. Based on recent studies using the Adult Attachment Interview, Zeanah and Zeanah have identified rejection, role reversal, and fear as major themes underlying different types of inner working models of individuals who were maltreated. Based on my own work, I would add emotionally unresponsive parenting as a major theme. My colleagues and I have identified a type of emotionally unresponsive parent that we call "psychologically unavailable"; we have found this form of maltreatment to have devastating effects on the development of young children.

One danger in attempting to view the intergenerational hypothesis from a pro or con perspective is the implication that there are only two points of view on this issue. It is not an "either/or" question. There are multiple etiologies of child maltreatment that have different impacts for each parent who maltreats his or her child. A history of maltreatment is one piece in this complex puzzle.

From the above review of the literature in the area of intergenerational transmission of child maltreatment, it seems safe to conclude that a history of having been maltreated is a major risk factor for maltreatment in the next generation. Many abusers were abused; however, many who were abused are providing good-quality care for their children. Rather than debating the validity of the intergenerational hypothesis of child abuse, we should be focusing on understanding the mechanism involved in the transmission of violence and how the cycle is broken. Perhaps we need further research to determine the exact rate of transmission, but clearly the research emphasis should be on determining the factors associated with breaking the cycle of abuse. Such a focus could lead eventually to effective prevention and intervention programs.

Chapter 3

How Can Society Respond to Child Abuse?

Chapter Preface

Experts offer various suggestions for how to prevent child abuse. Proposed measures include improved reporting methods, reforms of the foster care and adoption laws, and increased availability of drug and alcohol treatment for abusive parents. One of the most controversial ideas is to require parents to have licenses to raise children.

Proponents of parental licensure insist that many children are abused because their parents are incompetent. In order to ensure that such parents are not placed in a position to do harm to children, advocates insist, all parents and prospective parents should be required to undergo a licensing process and be certified as competent to care for children. Jack C. Westman, perhaps the most adamant supporter of parental licensure, explains, "A licensing process for parents would recognize parenting as a relationship sanctioned by society in the same sense that licensing marriage does. It would encourage people to become more responsible in their sexual behavior and in their rearing of children."

Opponents of parental licensure believe that such a policy would violate parents' rights by giving the government too much control over their personal decisions. As Charmaine Crouse Yoest, a fellow at the University of Virginia Department of Government and Foreign Affairs, argues, "In trying to combat child abuse, the state too often ends up addressing parents as if they are subordinates in an apprenticeship program. This attitude is clearly demonstrated in parent licensing proposals."

Parental licensing is just one of the issues debated in the following chapter on the prevention of child abuse.

Accurate Reporting Methods Are Needed to Combat Child Abuse

by Douglas J. Besharov and Lisa A. Laumann

About the authors: *Douglas J. Besharov is a visiting professor at the University of Maryland's School of Public Affairs. He is the author of* Recognizing Child Abuse: A Guide for the Concerned. *Lisa A. Laumann is pursuing a doctoral degree in clinical psychology at the University of Virginia.*

For 30 years, advocates, program administrators, and politicians have joined to encourage even more reports of suspected child abuse and neglect. Their efforts have been spectacularly successful, with about three million cases of suspected child abuse having been reported in 1993. Large numbers of endangered children still go unreported, but an equally serious problem has developed: Upon investigation, as many as 65 percent of the reports now being made are determined to be "unsubstantiated," raising serious civil liberties concerns and placing a heavy burden on already overwhelmed investigative staffs.

These two problems—nonreporting and inappropriate reporting—are linked and must be addressed together before further progress can be made in combating child abuse and neglect. To lessen both problems, there must be a shift in priorities—away from simply seeking more reports and toward encouraging better reports.

Reporting Laws

Since the early 1960s, all states have passed laws that require designated professionals to report specified types of child maltreatment. Over the years, both the range of designated professionals and the scope of reportable conditions have been steadily expanded.

Initially, mandatory reporting laws applied only to physicians, who were required to report only "serious physical injuries" and "nonaccidental injuries." In the ensuing years, however, increased public and professional attention, sparked in part by the number of abused children revealed by these initial reporting laws, led many states to expand their reporting requirements. Now almost all states have laws that require the reporting of all forms of suspected child mal-treatment, including physical abuse, physical neglect, emotional maltreatment, and, of course, sexual abuse and exploitation.

Under threat of civil and criminal penalties, these laws require most profes-sionals who serve children to report suspected child abuse and neglect. About twenty states require all citizens to report, but in every state, any citizen is per-mitted to report.

These reporting laws, associated public awareness campaigns, and profes-sional education programs have been strikingly successful. In 1993, there were about three million reports of children suspected of being abused or neglected. This is a twenty-fold increase since 1963, when about 150,000 cases were re-ported to the authorities. (As we will see, however, this figure is bloated by re-ports that later turn out to be unfounded.)

Many people ask whether this vast increase in reporting signals a rise in the incidence of child maltreatment. Recent increases in social problems such as out-of-wedlock births, inner-city poverty, and drug abuse have probably raised the underlying rates of child maltreatment, at least somewhat. Unfortunately, so many maltreated children previously went unreported that earlier reporting statistics do not provide a reliable baseline against which to make comparisons. One thing is clear, however: The great bulk of reports now received by child protective agencies would not be made but for the passage of mandatory report-ing laws and the media campaigns that accompanied them.

This increase in reporting was accompanied by a substantial expansion of prevention and treatment programs. Every community, for example, is now served by specialized child protective agencies that receive and investigate re-ports. Federal and state expenditures for child protective programs and associ-ated foster care services now exceed $6 billion a year. (Federal expenditures for foster care, child welfare, and related services make up less than 50 percent of total state and federal expenditures for these services; in 1992, they amounted to a total of $2,773.7 mil-lion. In addition, states may use a portion of the $2.8 billion federal So-cial Services Block Grant for such

> *"There must be a shift in [child abuse reporting] priorities— away from simply seeking more reports and toward encouraging better reports."*

services, though detailed data on these expenditures are not available. Begin-ning in 1994, additional federal appropriations funded family preservation and support services.)

As a result, many thousands of children have been saved from serious injury and even death. The best estimate is that over the past twenty years, child abuse and neglect deaths have fallen from over 3,000 a year—and perhaps as many as 5,000—to about 1,100 a year. In New York State, for example, within five years of the passage of a comprehensive reporting law, which also created specialized investigative staffs, there was a 50 percent reduction in child fatalities, from about two hundred a year to less than one hundred. (This is not meant to minimize the remaining problem. Even at this level, maltreatment is the sixth largest cause of death for children under fourteen.)

Unreported Cases

Most experts agree that reports have increased over the past thirty years because professionals and laypersons have become more likely to report apparently abusive and neglectful situations. But the question remains: How many more cases still go unreported?

Two studies performed for the National Center on Child Abuse and Neglect by Westat, Inc., provide a partial answer. In 1980 and then again in 1986, Westat conducted national studies of the incidence of child abuse and neglect. (A third Westat incidence study is now underway.) Each study used essentially the same methodology: In a stratified sample of counties, a broadly representative sample of professionals who serve children was asked whether, during the study period, the children they had seen in their professional capacities appeared to have been abused or neglected. (Actually, the professionals were not asked the ultimate question of whether the children appeared to be "abused" or "neglected." Instead, they were asked to identify children with certain, specified harms or conditions, which were then decoded into a count of various types of child abuse and neglect.) . . .

Westat found that professionals failed to report many of the children they saw who had observable signs of child abuse and neglect. Specifically, it found that in 1986, 56 percent of apparently abused or neglected children, or about 500,000 children, were not reported to the authorities. This figure, however, seems more alarming than it is: Basically, the more serious the case, the more likely the report. For example, the surveyed professionals reported over 85 percent of the fatal or serious physical abuse cases they saw, 72 percent of the sexual abuse cases, and 60 percent of the moderate physical abuse cases. In contrast, they only reported 15 percent of the educational neglect cases they saw, 24 percent of the emotional neglect cases, and 25 percent of the moderate physical neglect cases.

Nevertheless, there is no reason for complacency. Translating these raw percentages into actual cases means that in 1986, about 2,000 children with observable physical injuries severe enough to require hospitalization were not reported and that more than 100,000 children with moderate physical injuries went unreported, as did more than 30,000 apparently sexually abused children. And these are the rates of nonreporting among relatively well-trained professionals. One assumes that nonreporting is higher among less-well-trained professionals and higher still among laypersons.

Obtaining and maintaining a high level of reporting requires a continuation of the public education and professional training begun thirty years ago. But, now, such efforts must also address a problem as serious as nonreporting: inappropriate reporting.

At the same time that many seriously abused children go unreported, an equally serious problem further undercuts efforts to prevent child maltreatment: The nation's child protective agencies are being inundated by inappropriate reports. Although rules, procedures, and even terminology vary—some states use the phrase "unfounded," others "unsubstantiated" or "not indicated"—an "unfounded" report, in essence, is one that is dismissed after an investigation finds insufficient evidence upon which to proceed.

Unsubstantiated Reports

Nationwide, between 60 and 65 percent of all reports are closed after an initial investigation determines that they are "unfounded" or "unsubstantiated." This is in sharp contrast to 1974, when only about 45 percent of all reports were unfounded.

A few advocates, in a misguided effort to shield child protective programs from criticism, have sought to quarrel with estimates that I and others have made that the national unfounded rate is between 60 and 65 percent. They have grasped at various inconsistencies in the data collected by different organizations to claim either that the problem is not so bad or that it has always been this bad.

To help settle this dispute, the American Public Welfare Association (APWA) conducted a special survey of child welfare agencies in 1989. The APWA researchers found that between fiscal year 1986 and fiscal year 1988, the weighted average for the substantiation rates in thirty-one states declined 6.7 percent—from 41.8 percent in fiscal year 1986 to 39 percent in fiscal year 1988.

Most recently, the existence of this high unfounded rate was reconfirmed by the annual Fifty State Survey of the National Committee to Prevent Child Abuse (NCPCA), which found that in 1993 only about 34 percent of the reports received by child protective agencies were substantiated.

> *"The nation's child protective agencies are being inundated by inappropriate reports."*

The experience of New York City indicates what these statistics mean in practice. Between 1989 and 1993, as the number of reports received by the city's child welfare agency increased by over 30 percent (from 40,217 to 52,472), the percentage of substantiated reports fell by about 47 percent (from 45 percent to 24 percent). In fact, the number of substantiated cases—a number of families were reported more than once—actually fell by about 41 percent, from 14,026 to 8,326. Thus, 12,255 additional families were investigated, while 5,700 fewer families received child protective help.

The determination that a report is unfounded can only be made after an unavoidably traumatic investigation that is inherently a breach of parental and family privacy. To determine whether a particular child is in danger, caseworkers must inquire into the most intimate personal and family matters. Often it is necessary to question friends, relatives, and neighbors, as well as school teachers, day-care personnel, doctors, clergy, and others who know the family.

> *"Each year, about 700,000 families are put through investigations of unfounded reports."*

Laws against child abuse are an implicit recognition that family privacy must give way to the need to protect helpless children. But in seeking to protect children, it is all too easy to ignore the legitimate rights of parents. Each year, about 700,000 families are put through investigations of unfounded reports. This is a massive and unjustified violation of parental rights.

Few unfounded reports are made maliciously. Studies of sexual abuse reports, for example, suggest that, at most, from 4 to 10 percent of these reports are knowingly false. Many involve situations in which the person reporting, in a well-intentioned effort to protect a child, overreacts to a vague and often misleading possibility that the child may be maltreated. Others involve situations of poor child care that, though of legitimate concern, simply do not amount to child abuse or neglect. In fact, a substantial proportion of unfounded cases are referred to other agencies for them to provide needed services for the family.

Moreover, an unfounded report does not necessarily mean that the child was not actually abused or neglected. Evidence of child maltreatment is hard to obtain and might not be uncovered when agencies lack the time and resources to complete a thorough investigation or when inaccurate information is given to the investigator. Other cases are labeled unfounded when no services are available to help the family. Some cases must be closed because the child or family cannot be located.

A certain proportion of unfounded reports, therefore, is an inherent—and legitimate—aspect of reporting suspected child maltreatment and is necessary to ensure adequate child protection. Hundreds of thousands of strangers report their suspicions; they cannot all be right. But unfounded rates of the current magnitude go beyond anything reasonably needed. Worse, they endanger children who are really abused.

The current flood of unfounded reports is overwhelming the limited resources of child protective agencies. For fear of missing even one abused child, workers perform extensive investigations of vague and apparently unsupported reports. Even when a home visit based on an anonymous report turns up no evidence of maltreatment, they usually interview neighbors, school teachers, and day-care personnel to make sure that the child is not abused. And even repeated anonymous and unfounded reports do not prevent a further investigation. But all this takes time.

As a result, children in real danger are getting lost in the press of inappropriate cases. Forced to allocate a substantial portion of their limited resources to unfounded reports, child protective agencies are less able to respond promptly and effectively when children are in serious danger. Some reports are left uninvestigated for a week and even two weeks after they are received. Investigations often miss key facts, as workers rush to clear cases, and dangerous home situations receive inadequate supervision, as workers must ignore pending cases as they investigate the new reports that arrive daily on their desks. Decision making also suffers. With so many cases of unsubstantiated or unproven risk to children, caseworkers are desensitized to the obvious warning signals of immediate and serious danger.

> *"Children in real danger are getting lost in the press of inappropriate cases."*

These nationwide conditions help explain why from 25 to 50 percent of child abuse deaths involve children previously known to the authorities. In 1993, the NCPCA reported that of the 1,149 child maltreatment deaths, 42 percent had already been reported to the authorities. Tens of thousands of other children suffer serious injuries short of death while under child protective agency supervision. . . .

Shifting Priorities

The emotionally charged desire to "do something" about child abuse, fanned by repeated and often sensational media coverage, has led to an understandable but counterproductive overreaction on the part of the professionals and citizens who report suspected child abuse. For thirty years, advocates, program administrators, and politicians have all pushed for more reporting of suspected child abuse and neglect.

Potential reporters are frequently told to "take no chances" and to report any child for whom they have the slightest concern. There is a recent tendency to tell people to report children whose behavior suggests that they may have been abused—even in the absence of any other evidence of maltreatment. These "behavioral indicators" include, for example, children who are unusually withdrawn or shy as well as children who are unusually friendly to strangers. However, only a small minority of children who exhibit such behaviors have actually been maltreated.

Thirty years ago, even fifteen years ago, when many professionals were construing their reporting obligations narrowly to avoid taking action to protect endangered children, this approach may have been needed. Now, though, all it does is ensure that child abuse hotlines will be flooded with inappropriate and unfounded reports.

Few people fail to report because they do not care about an endangered child. Instead, they may be unaware of the danger the child faces or of the protective procedures that are available. A study of nonreporting among teachers, for example, blamed their "lack of knowledge for detecting symptoms of child abuse and neglect." Likewise, few inappropriate or unfounded reports are deliberately false statements. Most involve an honest desire to protect children coupled with confusion about what conditions are reportable.

Confusion about reporting is largely caused by the vagueness of reporting laws and aggravated by the failure of child protective agencies to provide realistic guidance about deciding to report. In 1987, a national group of thirty-eight child protection professionals from nineteen states met for three days at Airlie House, Virginia, under the auspices of the American Bar Association's National Legal Resource Center for Child Advocacy and Protection in association with the American Public Welfare Association and the American Enterprise Institute. The "Airlie House group," as it has come to be called, developed policy guidelines for reporting and investigative decision making. (I was the rapporteur for the effort.) One of the group's major conclusions was that "better public and professional materials are needed to obtain more appropriate reporting." The group specifically recommended that "educational materials and programs should: (1) clarify the legal definitions of child abuse and neglect, (2) give general descriptions of reportable situations (including specific examples), and (3) explain what to expect when a report is made. Brochures and other materials for laypersons, including public service announcements, should give specific information about what to report—and what not to report."

Based on these recommendations, a relatively clear agenda for reform emerges; we must

> *"Existing [child abuse reporting] laws are often vague and overbroad."*

Clarify child abuse reporting laws.
Existing laws are often vague and overbroad. They should be rewritten to provide real guidance about what conditions should and should not be reported. This can be accomplished without radically departing from present laws or practices. The key is to describe reportable conditions in terms of specific parental behaviors or conditions that are tied to severe and demonstrable harms (or potential harms) to children.

It would help, for example, to make a distinction between direct evidence, meaning firsthand accounts or observations of seriously harmful parental behavior, and circumstantial evidence, meaning concrete facts, such as the child's physical condition, that suggest that the child has been abused or neglected. Behavioral indicators, however, should not by themselves be considered a sufficient basis for a report.

Direct evidence includes eyewitness observations of a parent's abusive or neglectful behavior; the child's description of being abused or neglected, unless there is a specific reason for disbelief; the parent's own description of abusive or neglectful behavior, unless it is long past; accounts of child maltreatment from spouses or other family members; films, photographs, or other visual material depicting sexually explicit activity by a minor; newborns denied nutrition, life-sustaining care, or other medically indicated treatment; children in physically dangerous situations; young children left alone; apparently abandoned children; demonstrated parental disabilities (for example, mental illness or retardation or alcohol or drug abuse) severe enough to make child abuse or child neglect likely; and demonstrated parental inability to care for a newborn baby.

> *"Appropriate reporting of suspected child maltreatment requires a sophisticated knowledge of many legal, administrative, and diagnostic matters."*

Circumstantial evidence includes "suspicious" injuries suggesting physical abuse; physical injuries or medical findings suggesting sexual abuse; for young children, signs of sexual activity; signs of severe physical deprivation on the child's body suggesting general child neglect; severe dirt and disorder in the home suggesting general child neglect; apparently untreated physical injuries, illnesses, or impairments suggesting medical neglect; "accidental" injuries suggesting gross inattention to the child's need for safety; apparent parental indifference to a child's severe psychological or developmental problems; apparent parental condonation of or indifference to a child's misbehavior suggesting improper ethical guidance; chronic and unexplained absences from school suggesting parental responsibility for the nonattendance; and newborns showing signs of fetal exposure to drugs or alcohol.

Provide continuing public education and professional training. Few people fail to report because they want children to suffer abuse and neglect. Likewise, few people make deliberately false reports. Most involve an honest desire to protect children coupled with confusion about what conditions are reportable. Thus, educational efforts should emphasize the conditions that do not justify a report, as well as those that do.

Screen reports. No matter how well professionals are trained and no matter how extensive public education efforts are, there will always be a tendency for persons to report cases that should not be investigated. Until recently, most states did not have formal policies and procedures for determining whether to accept a call for investigation. Such policies should be adopted by all states and they should provide explicit guidance about the kinds of cases that should not be assigned for investigation.

Reports should be rejected when the allegations fall outside the agency's definitions of "child abuse" and "child neglect" as established by state law. Often, the family has a coping problem for which they would be more appropriately referred to another social service agency. (Prime examples include children beyond the specified age, alleged perpetrators falling outside the legal definition, and family problems not amounting to child maltreatment.) Reports should also be rejected when the caller can give no credible reason for suspecting that the child has been abused or neglected. (Although actual proof of the maltreatment is not required, some evidence is.) Reports whose unfounded or malicious nature is established by specific evidence, of course, should also be rejected. (Anonymous reports, reports from estranged spouses, and even previous unfounded reports from the same source should not be automatically rejected, but they need to be carefully evaluated.) And, finally, reports in which insufficient information is given to identify or locate the child should likewise be screened (although the information may be kept for later use if a subsequent report about the same child is made).

In questionable circumstances, the agency should recontact the caller before deciding to reject a report. When appropriate, rejected reports should be referred to other agencies that can provide services needed by the family.

Modify liability laws. Current laws provide immunity for anyone who makes a report in good faith but give no protection to those who, in a good-faith exercise of professional judgment, decide that a child has not been abused or neglected and hence should not be reported. This combination of immunities and penalties encourages the overreporting of questionable situations.

Give feedback to persons who report. If persons who report are not told what happened, they may conclude that the agency's response was ineffective or even harmful to the child, and the next time they suspect that a child is maltreated, they may decide not to report. In addition, finding out whether their suspicions were valid also refines their diagnostic skills and thus improves the quality and accuracy of their future reports. Reporters also need such information to interpret subsequent events and to monitor the child's conditions.

Adopt an agency policy. Appropriate reporting of suspected child maltreatment requires a sophisticated knowledge of many legal, administrative, and diagnostic matters. To help ensure that their staffs respond properly, an increasing number of public and private agencies are adopting formal agency policies about reporting. Some state laws mandate them. The primary purpose of these policies, or agency protocols, is to inform staff members of their obligation to report and of the procedures to be followed. Such formal policies serve another important function: They are an implicit commitment by agency administrators to support frontline staff members who decide to report. Moreover, the very process of drafting a written document can clarify previously ambiguous or ill-conceived agency policies.

Parents Should Be Licensed

by Jack C. Westman

About the author: *Jack C. Westman is a professor of psychiatry at the University of Wisconsin at Madison, and editor of* Child Psychiatry and Human Development.

In spite of the frequently heard phrase "children are our most precious national resource," our actions and inactions speak otherwise. At the root of this misfortune are the lack of recognition of the civil right of children to competent parenting and the lack of enforcement of the legal right of children to be protected from incompetent parenting.

Anyone who conceives and gives birth to a child is entitled to raise that child and may be entitled to receive governmental financial and possibly educational support. No one asks if that person is capable of parenting that child.

This situation results from popular views of parenthood that emphasize the freedom of adults to do as they wish and that emphasize the privacy of family life. Those views really regard children as the property of their parents. The principle of a child's interests and the principle of the common good of society are seldom applied to family life.

The United States is the only Western nation that does not significantly accommodate the workplace or governmental finance to the responsibilities of parenting. There is no credible statement of our society's interest in rearing children to become competent citizens. More significantly, there is little recognition of the connection between our social problems and incompetent parenting.

The Social Costs of Incompetent Parenting

The enormous financial and human costs of incompetent parenting, especially for high-risk, disadvantaged children are beginning to come to light at two levels.

The first level is the professional recognition that adult criminal recidivism and intergenerational welfare dependency are products of incompetent parenting, and that competent parenting protects even the biologically vulnerable and socioeconomically disadvantaged from those adult outcomes.

The second level is the growing public awareness of the obvious damage to children from the abuse, neglect, and sexually transmitted diseases of incompetent parents. This was signaled in 1991 by the National Commission on Children, appointed by Congress and by the President. The Commission called attention to the growing number of mothers and fathers who lack both the commitment and the ability to be competent parents. . . .

Most children who live in poverty, most children who come from "broken" homes, most children who receive welfare, most children who have been abused, and most children who have criminal relatives do not become habitual criminals or chronic welfare cases. When any of these factors converge with parental neglect, however, a significant number of children are destined for criminality or welfare dependency. This happens because these children do not learn how to relate to other people and to become responsible citizens.

We now can add incompetent parenting to the list of factors that adversely affect the development of children. The past exclusive focus on socioeconomic, racial, educational, marital, gender, biological, and ecological factors has obscured the most important and obvious element in child development—parenting. The time to help children is before and as their problems appear by redressing incompetent parenting, not after damage has been done. We cannot be reassured by the fact that some adults succeed in life in spite or because of childhood adversity; the vast majority do not. Incompetent parenting is a damaging reality that society can no longer afford to ignore, much less support.

Our Society Must Value Parenting

Because we already have statutes that mandate intervention in families in which child abuse and neglect take place, you might ask why we need to do more.

The answer is that our present approach is dominated by juvenile ageism and does not recognize the basic human and civil rights of children. Our society sets no positive standards for parenting and requires damage to children before it intervenes. Because there are no articulated expectations of parents before they damage their children, we place the responsibility on our government to protect children after abuse and neglect have occurred rather than on parents to refrain from damaging their children in the first place. . . .

> *"There is little recognition of the connection between our social problems and incompetent parenting."*

Our society must clearly state that competent parenting is essential to our democratic way of life and ultimately to the preservation of our species. When the sole emphasis of solutions to social problems is technological in the form of increasing professional services, education, and financial aid, the call for society's valuation of parenting is obscured. Because there has been no national recognition that competent parenting is vital to the integrity of our society, social services for families and education for children actually have deteriorated. The effectiveness of services for children and families depends upon a supportive social context that values parenting. Because persuasion and education in themselves are insufficient measures to ensure general compliance with a social value, parenting needs to be accorded a legal status that recognizes the reciprocal obligations of parents and children to each other. . . .

Social Welfare Is Not Enough

Although social welfare policies in the United States have been successful in many respects, few question the need for reform in our welfare system and in our approach to poverty. The programs implemented and expanded during the War on Poverty era reshaped our social safety net. As bad as the child poverty situation is now, it would be more severe if there were no programs such as Head Start, food stamps, basic educational opportunity grants, Medicare, Medicaid, and low income energy assistance.

Still, a new concept of public welfare is sorely needed. The polarized images of the poor as being either lazy and exploitative or downtrodden and exploited tend to block constructive changes. This polarization is expressed in the views that either the poor themselves or "the system" are the problems. Missing are means of ensuring that opportunities for self-improvement are available to all citizens, including the socioeconomically disadvantaged. . . .

> *"Incompetent parenting is a damaging reality that society can no longer afford to ignore."*

The main issue is no longer how much to do for the poor but whether and how much to require them to do in return for support. The federal government is moving in the direction of linking accountability to the receipt of financial support. This has taken the form of expecting welfare recipients to obtain training and to be employed to the extent of their abilities. Recipients are expected to contribute to their own support and to manage public assistance responsibly. Consistent with this trend, eligibility for aid to the parents of dependent children could be based upon ensuring the recipients' minimal competence as parents through a licensing process. . . .

The Need for a National Parenting Policy

The current plight of our children could be a stimulus for our society to heal itself by dealing with the institutional defects of our society—inadequate schools, housing, public welfare, control of violence and disorder, and ethics in government. That healing could take place if we devote our attention to articulating our societal and cultural objectives for our citizens by expecting and supporting competence in the parenting of our children. The ability to cooperate with others resulting from competent parenting is essential to the survival of individuals in a modern, democratic society—indeed, to the survival of individual freedom itself.

The societal objectives of childrearing in the United States are to produce competent, productive consumers, who also are educated citizens. The American cultural childrearing objectives are to produce autonomous, responsible persons capable of self-fulfillment and of contributing to the common good.

> *"Our society must clearly state that competent parenting is essential to our democratic way of life and ultimately to the preservation of our species."*

The United States has not clearly recognized that competent parenting is an essential foundation for competent citizenship. This is a reflection of juvenile ageism—the subtle, but profound, prejudice and discrimination against children, particularly for the disadvantaged where it is compounded by racism and sexism. Because of juvenile ageism our society operates as though children do not have human and civil rights.

When the repercussions of juvenile ageism are faced, we can begin to find ways to accord children the same civil right expected by adults: the opportunity to be free of insurmountable barriers to the pursuit of developing one's talents in life. This can be done by asking if public and private programs for children strengthen or weaken the child-parent affectionate attachment bond and if they strengthen or undermine parenting. This can be done by according legal status to parenting as a simple, but clear, expression by society that parenting is to be taken seriously as a privilege rather than as a biological right.

A national policy for supporting parenting could target our resources on promoting, supporting, and expecting competent parenting and the converse of identifying, remediating, and, when necessary, replacing incompetent parenting. Its repercussions would extend throughout society by recognizing that parenting is as important to society as is remunerated employment.

Because it would mean preparing young people for parenthood, the national objective of competent parenting for all children would focus attention on the importance of providing an adequate education for everyone. Because poverty is harmful to children, it would focus attention on the socioeconomically disadvantaged segments of the population. Because the demands of childrearing and employment away from home often conflict, it also would focus attention on the importance of accommodating the workplace to parenting.

Implementing a Parenting Policy Through Licensure

At the level of the states, a national parenting policy could be implemented by licensing parents. By doing so the United States would lead other nations in according civil rights to children and, because few will admit to being against the interests of children, would further enhance respect for human rights in general.

A licensing process for parents would recognize parenting as a relationship sanctioned by society in the same sense that licensing marriage does. It would encourage people to become more responsible in their sexual behavior and in their rearing of children. It would focus public policies on supporting competent parenting and on remedying or replacing incompetent parenting.

> *"A licensing process for parents would recognize parenting as a relationship sanctioned by society in the same sense that licensing marriage does."*

Important in all of these considerations are value judgments based upon the civil rights inherent in American culture: that every individual, regardless of sex, race, or age, should have the opportunity to pursue life, liberty, and happiness. In order to realize these ideals, there are times when the interests of society must take precedence over a particular individual's wishes or emotional state. One of those times is when an incompetent parent interferes with a child's opportunity to develop in life so as to become a competent adult.

Any effort to help children and foundering parents must have clear and measurable objectives. It is not enough to draw upon charitable impulses or appeals for social justice. Furthermore, simply increasing income or the employment of parents are not sufficient objectives, because they do not necessarily directly benefit the target of the aid—the children. Objectives based on the principles that each child has a right to competent parenting and a right to be protected from incompetent parenting would insure that children are helped.

Even if the licensing of parents were never implemented, debates about it would focus public attention on the importance of parenting and would bring expressions of concern about children down from abstract rhetoric to reality. It would expose juvenile ageism. It would call attention to the political disenfranchisement of children and the possibility of supporting parenting through such means as parents casting votes for their children. . . .

Although inevitable conflicts exist between the interests of older and younger generations, it seems that America's latent will is to promote the healthy development of all of our children. The problem lies in finding feasible ways to do so. If we do nothing to protect our children from abuse and neglect, future generations will wonder how we permitted anyone to rear children without considering their competence to do so. They will know the consequences of ignoring incompetent parents until they irretrievably damage our children and our society.

Parental Licensure Is Dangerous

by **Charmaine Crouse Yoest**

About the author: *Charmaine Crouse Yoest is an author and a Bradley Fellow at the University of Virginia.*

Imagine for a moment. It's a quiet, suburban neighborhood with children playing in the *cul de sac*. An earnest-looking investigator from the state's Child Protective Services department approaches one of the homes and knocks on the door; a young woman answers. The investigator says, "I'm from Child Protective Services. I need to see your license." He means her parenting license. Debra Wilson had obtained the license in order to qualify for the child income tax deduction. The Wilsons needed every penny, since Debra's husband Steve had been unemployed for six months after a wave of downsizing at his company.

That decision led to a web of unforeseen government interventions with lasting consequences in the Wilsons' life. The licensing application had flagged the family as "at-risk" because of Steve's unemployment. Soon, a home educator from the state came to offer enrollment in the Parents as Teachers program; it seemed like a good idea at the time because the young woman guided them toward free services in the community that helped during their financial crunch. What the Wilsons didn't know was that, during Stacy Kennedy's year of periodic visits to their home, where she was greeted as a friend, she had been compiling a list of the family's "risk factors."

Now it was all there in a permanent file with the Child Protective Services. Even though Stacy was young and had no children herself, she had murmured sympathetically when Deb chatted about her frustration over not losing weight after the birth of her fourth child. Being too heavy: *risk factor*. Then there was the day her allergies were really acting up. Stacy was so helpful, recommending a new brand of inhalers, but allergies are a *risk factor*. Then there was the day she showed up just after Deb found out her father had died suddenly. How comforting to have a friend's shoulder to cry on, but death in the family is a *risk fac-*

Excerpted from Charmaine Crouse Yoest, "Beyond *1984*," available at www.frc.org/insight/is97f4pa.html. Reprinted with permission from the Family Research Council.

tor. Everyone was overjoyed when Steve got his new job—the downsizing turned out to be a blessing in disguise. His new job was a career advancement with a larger salary. Unfortunately, Deb happened to mention that he would be traveling frequently. *Risk factor.* Then there was the day when Stacy showed up unexpectedly and, well, Deb was having a bad day. When Deb told Steve about it that night it seemed kind of funny: she was in her bathrobe when the doorbell rang just as she'd finished spanking Bobby for hitting Betsy while they were fighting over a toy, and baby Monique was screaming because of all the commotion, and the breakfast dishes were still on the table. Spanking is a *risk factor*, and, since the baby had been crying last time Stacy visited, too, she thought perhaps that Deb was unable to "understand the baby's cues." Another *risk factor*.

They were so excited when Catherine, the Wilsons' oldest daughter, was accepted into a magnet school. The Parent-Teacher Contract they were required to sign seemed odd, but Stacy encouraged them to sign. It required Deb and Steve to serve forty hours of "volunteer" work. By the mid-year mark, they had only completed ten hours, and the experience had been trying. They had baby-sat a teacher's children. The two boys had been careless with the Wilsons' things, breaking a lamp and spilling grape juice on the light beige carpet, among other things. They were impossible to discipline, as they showed no respect for authority, and the Wilsons were strictly forbidden from imposing any corporal punishment. Worse, some negative comments from the boys about the Wilsons' family life (they let their kids stay up too late too often) had also been added to that growing *risk factor* file.

Now, the family's life was being inspected for possible revocation of their parenting license; they knew not why.

Parents Rights vs. States Rights

Every element of this Orwellian scenario either is in place or has been proposed somewhere in this nation. Parent licensing isn't imminent in our country, but proposals for licensing, and for its close cousin—parent training—keep working their way into the elite debate over education and family issues. While this debate goes on at the policy-maker level, the effect of a pernicious state nannyism has trickled down to influence the lives of average Americans and their children. For example, the national Parent Teacher Association (PTA) has a position statement on parental involvement that "points out parents' rights and responsibilities as well as PTA responsibilities and *rights* in protecting the education, health and well-being of the whole child" (emphasis ours).

> *"Proposals for [parent] licensing, and for its close cousin—parent training—keep working their way into the elite debate over education and family issues."*

Parents find themselves uncomfortably operating in a world where it seems everyone from the PTA to the pediatrician has "rights" over their children. Wording in the 1994 federal legislation reauthorizing the Elementary and Secondary Education Act is telling. In Section 1118, titled "Parental Involvement," the law states that each school shall "educate teachers . . . in the value and utility of contributions of parents . . . and work with parents *as equal partners*, implement and coordinate parent programs, and build ties between home and school." (emphasis ours).

Under the watchful Clinton administration, federal education policy has gradually eroded the authority of parents. Clearly, even the common understanding of parents' rights has changed. They are now, at best, first among equals as authority figures in their children's lives in the global village. In education jargon, parents are now merely "stakeholders," along with business, state and community.

There are many different streams of a turbulent society coming together to form this river of change. The rising tide of family breakdown, single parenthood, and increased reports of child abuse undermine the traditional American respect for the rights of the nuclear family. Every report of an abused child is horrifying and leads to the thought: *there's got to be something that can be done*. That *something* in the age of Mrs. Clinton's "village" usually means state action. At the same time, plummeting levels of educational achievement have highlighted one of the reasons why we so need the family. Falling test scores bring more calls for parental involvement in the schools. Once again, the state hears a siren call to action.

> *"Parents find themselves uncomfortably operating in a world where it seems everyone from the PTA to the pediatrician has 'rights' over their children."*

One scenario provides a negative justification for expanded societal action—to prevent child neglect and abuse—and the other provides a positive justification—to promote greater parental involvement in their children's education. Either way, the evolving philosophy views the state (and its agents, the schools) as the supervisor of the family, rather than its servant. On the practical level, this philosophy provides a rationale for expansion of paternalistic approaches to parents. . . .

Legal Foundations

The epicenter of state involvement with parents is the public school. Public education provides the field for competing interests to play out the clash between parents' rights and state interference with regard to the children. In American history, this clash is relatively new. Common sense and the law have until recently agreed that parents are the ones who have the right to direct their children's education. This is, the Supreme Court has said, "an enduring American tradition."

In this century, however, a new philosophy rivals that tradition. The nanny state now has its own body of case law that has established the state's "rights" in educating children. The development of compulsory school attendance, child labor laws, and mandatory immunization have provided a bulwark for the state's "rights" over children. These popularly supported issues have spread to include a host of legal battles over religious expression in schools, curriculum content, and sex education, including dispensing of contraceptive devices. In these battles, the state has some powerful precedent on its side. In *Prince v. Massachusetts*, a child labor case, the Supreme Court declared, "The family itself is not beyond regulation in the public interest. . . . And neither rights of religion nor rights of parenthood are beyond limitation."

> *"The development of compulsory school attendance, child labor laws, and mandatory immunization have provided a bulwark for the state's 'rights' over children."*

Deborah and Terry Dawson, of Houston, Texas, experienced this first-hand. Their son Bradley told a school counselor that his parents had paddled him. Subsequently, the Harris County Children's Protective Services sent an investigator to Bradley's school to interview him without the Dawsons' knowledge. A female investigator forced him to strip so that she could examine him for evidence of the paddling. She then instructed him to lie to his parents so that they would not find out about the interview. The Dawsons sued and lost. Federal District Judge Melinda Harmon, who ruled on the case, strongly implied that parents give up their rights when they drop off their children at public school.

Parent Licensing: A New Paradigm for Parenting

The Dawson case illustrates the underlying issues that form the tension surrounding the advocacy of parental licensing. The concern over protecting children from abuse is legitimate. However, in trying to combat child abuse, the state too often ends up addressing parents as if they are subordinates in an apprenticeship program. This attitude is clearly demonstrated in parent licensing proposals. "A parent license would place the responsibility on parents to be competent," explains Jack C. Westman, a psychiatrist at the University of Wisconsin and, as author of *Licensing Parents: Can We Prevent Child Abuse and Neglect?*, one of the most prominent licensing advocates. "The burden of proof would be on parents to demonstrate that they are not abusing and neglecting their children rather than on the state to prove through quasi-criminal proceedings that parents are unfit after they have damaged their children."

Westman writes passionately and insistently about the awesome responsibilities of parents and the social importance of "competent parenting." "We need a new paradigm in which parenthood is a privilege," he writes. "It is a divine obligation when parenthood is viewed as a covenant with God." Willing to invoke God's role, Westman nonetheless undermines parental authority in the details of his proposals.

Westman says, "Society must engender . . . the awareness of what it is to be a good parent." But it is not society as much as it is government which has the power to define good parenting and punish bad parenting. For example, Westman himself doesn't appear to notice that, even within his proposal, he has already redefined traditional standards for parenting: an age threshold—eighteen—is given as a standard for parenting eligibility, not marriage. His licenses would be given out to individuals, not married couples. The complications would only grow from there. What will the definition of *abuse* be? There are those who see child abuse around every corner. Doris Wild Helmering, a psychotherapist, writes, "You can abuse a child in many other ways than actively hitting, pushing, pinching and name-calling." Included in her page-long list of forms of "passive abuse" is "Neglecting to fill out your child's school forms."

Westman presents a relatively benign portrait of licensing, purposefully cautioning that it would only negatively affect a small number of "incompetent parents." Some of his peers are unapologetically draconian. David Lykken, author of *Antisocial Personalities*, has similarly advocated parental licensing as a way to address sociopathy. He has called for immediately removing newborns from the custody of unlicensed mothers so that they can be placed directly into foster homes and quickly adopted.

These licensing proposals themselves are not directly education issues or school-related. However, licensing is a natural extension of, and is easily connected to, increased calls for parent education and parent training, the nexus of which is the place

> *"In trying to combat child abuse, the state too often ends up addressing parents as if they are subordinates in an apprenticeship program."*

where parents can most easily be found: the schools. Indeed, Westman himself comments: "Education in parenting is important and should be made available in the schools and to all parents who desire it." He outlines a very detailed and specific procedure for licensing parents which includes three criteria for licensure. The third criterion is:

> Possession of basic knowledge of child-rearing, such as by completing a parenting course in a school or clinic or its equivalent. In all likelihood, parent licensing would stimulate the development of family life education, already offered in many communities. . . . From the point of view of the educational curriculum, preparation for parenthood is more important than any other academic subject. . . .

As we cross that "bridge to the 21st century," we go beyond *1984* in more ways than one. Will our schools be equal to the challenge of educating the next generation? Ironically, rather than tackling that question, the school of the 21st century is being strategically crafted as a one-stop social welfare agency—precisely at a time that the educational demands of our society are escalating. The educational establishment is grabbing new paternalistic powers, and usurping parents' rights, without fulfilling its fundamental mission of teaching our children.

A new paradigm of parenting is indeed coming into play, so subtly that it is imperceptible to the average parent caught up in the everyday details of family life. Buried in federal code, unheralded in the headlines, unbeknownst to moms and dads across the country, education bureaucrats have become "equal partners" with parents. Recognizing resistance from parents who take seriously their obligation to raise their own children, liberal advocates have stressed their support for parental "involvement" in the schools. This involvement, however, would better have been described by today's liberals during their radical student days as "co-opting" parents. Such involvement as the education establishment has permitted parents has usually taken the form of meeting-going, form-filling, and in-school volunteering. Seldom are parents *involved* in curriculum, discipline, and finance decisions. As one wit has described it: "The children of Israel were very *involved* in the building of the pyramids, but they had no *authority* over the project."

Enervating rather than empowering, "parental involvement" and "equal partners" language lies silently on the page, forming the foundation for the school of the 21st century. Left unchallenged, it will prove the undoing of family privacy, parental authority, and individual rights in the 21st century.

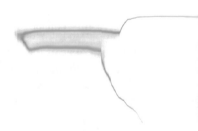

Family Preservation Laws Must Be Reformed

by Kellye R. Wood

About the author: *Kellye R. Wood is a preschool teacher in Six Lakes, Michigan.*

For the past decade or so, child-protection officials in Michigan, like those in most states, have followed a mandate to preserve families and avoid placing children in foster homes whenever possible. In Michigan's Families First program, a caseworker provides troubled families several weeks of intense intervention. The idea behind Families First appeals both to conservatives, who don't want the government breaking up families, and to liberals, who don't believe society should impose "middle-class values" on the poor.

The Cost of Families First

But those of us who work directly with children—I have taught kindergarten and preschool in Michigan public schools for seven years—witness the results of this social experiment. And for an abused child left in a high-risk home, those results can be tragic—as I saw when I taught kindergarten in a small northern Michigan town.

One boy came to school in 15-degree weather wearing a pair of old tennis shoes and no socks. The school got him socks and boots, but one week later, the liners were rotting wet and he was again sockless. Nobody at home was helping him. The boy told us he "couldn't find no socks" because his mother was sleeping when he got ready for school. His family had a history of reports to the child-protection agency, dating from when his older siblings entered school. The caseworker told us that the boy's mother needed someone to "stay on her," because she "backslides," doing things like leaving the children alone at night. A caseworker, we were promised, would teach Mother how to care for her children—again. The school came up with its own remedy: a shoe box full of clean socks, which we kept in the classroom for the youngster.

A girl came to school one day with choke marks; she described how Mommy got mad and grabbed her neck. This girl often arrived at school extremely with-

Reprinted from Kellye R. Wood, "Stop Sacrificing Children to 'Save' Families," *The Wall Street Journal*, March 13, 1997. Reprinted with permission from the author.

drawn, then pathetically grateful for attention. At the parent-teacher conference, her mother talked about wanting to "just get rid" of the girl. A Families First caseworker worked with the family; three years later, the girl's current teacher says she's doing as well as one could expect—given her home situation.

Consistent, Loving Care

Before Families First, children seemed to be removed from dangerous homes sooner. In foster families their physical care improved. They came to school rested, fed and better able to learn. The presence of consistent, loving care in their lives more than offset the harm of separation from their biological families. Under Families First, children seem more likely to be returned to homes where "tough love" takes on a terrifying meaning.

Even in the worst cases of abuse, it is heartbreakingly difficult to remove a child from a bad home. One boy in my class had been physically and sexually abused by his father with his mother's knowledge. He was taken from his home; his father ended up in prison. By kindergarten, the boy had lived with his foster "Grandma" and "Grandpa" for two years. Yet although visits with his mother disturbed the boy, the authorities ultimately returned him to her and her boyfriend for one more try. He began coming to school wearing dirty clothes that smelled of cat urine. His behavior was erratic, punctuated by high pitched giggling and bursts of running. When it turned out he had been chained to a chair, he

> *"Even in the worst cases of abuse, it is heartbreakingly difficult to remove a child from a bad home."*

was permanently removed, at last. The last I heard the boy was living with a loving couple who hoped to adopt him. But the damage had been done. At five years of age, this child functioned like a three-year-old.

Abused children expend their energies surviving, not learning. That's a common-sense notion validated by brain research, which shows that extreme stress in early childhood permanently impairs the development of mental "circuits." A child who endures years of abuse is likely to be left with a poorer intellect and a diminished potential to learn.

Restoring Balance to the System

The sad truth is that some parents will never or can never care for their children in even a minimal way. It's time to bring some balance back to the child-protection system. I suggest something akin to "three times and out" for child abuse or neglect, meaning that children would be removed from homes after a set number of interventions. No child should be deprived of the basic right to grow up safely.

The costs of Families First mount daily: for the child who misses weeks of school, unable to return until her parent gets her (often free) immunizations; for the child who precisely describes how to use a "bong" during a field trip to the police station; for the child who describes sex acts in explicit detail; for the child with bruises from an angry parent; for the child who tells about drunken parents at sharing time; for the child disciplined by being thrown out in a snowbank without a coat; for the child who wears her bathing suit for underwear and summer clothing in the dead of winter—for all the children whose chances at life are eroded in countless little and big ways each day.

I have seen the daily toll that chronic abuse extracts on the spirits and bodies of young kids. I believe in keeping families together, but not when it means sacrificing children. There are signs that the pendulum is beginning to swing in Michigan: the lieutenant governor's Children's Commission, Governor John Engler's endorsement of the commission's work in his State of the State address, a Children's Ombudsman's report and a stated priority to protect children from the incoming director of the Family Independence Agency.

For the children's sake, let's get it right this time. The standard should be "Who can provide basic care or keep a child physically safe?" Abused and neglected children can grow up to be contributing citizens—or they can become their parents. As a society, we can perpetuate the cycle or break it. The choice is ours through the policies that we shape.

The Adoption of Abused Children Must Be Made Easier

by Art Moore

About the author: *Art Moore is a contributor to* Christianity Today.

Angelica Hubbard's six-year odyssey—from a Los Angeles emergency room, where she arrived eight weeks after birth with broken bones and brain damage, to the security and nurture of her adoptive family—reveals in stark detail how the foster-care system can harm as much as it helps.

"Over the past 20 years a whole state of limbo has come into existence where no judgment is made, where the child is neither fish nor fowl," says Patrick Fagan, senior fellow in family and cultural issues at the Heritage Foundation in Washington, D.C. "He's neither, as it were, the proper child of his parents who are raising him well, nor has he become the adoptive child of somebody else who is going to raise him well. Instead he's the ward of the courts, and he's bounced frequently from one foster home to another to another."

In 1991, Los Angeles County placed Angelica through a private agency in the home of Doug and Kathy Hubbard, an American Baptist youth minister and his wife. The couple gingerly embraced Angelica for the first time in a hospital room, where tests revealed bone fractures and neurological damage. For the next five years, Angelica was at the mercy of a state system, which put the rights of her birth parents ahead of her needs.

Eventually, Angelica's Hispanic birth parents satisfied state requirements and she returned to her original home at age two. But six months later, Angelica was back in a hospital, malnourished and with bruises and bite marks. From jail, her birth mother telephoned her case worker and pleaded for Angelica to be sent to the Hubbards. The agency rejected her appeal and placed the child with another Hispanic family. "To Angelica we were Mommy and Daddy, but their answer was, She's already been placed; we can't tell you any more," Kathy Hubbard says.

Excerpted from Art Moore, "Can Foster Care Be Fixed?" *Christianity Today*, August 10, 1998. Reprinted with permission from the author.

Yet the Hubbards were determined and contacted the new foster family, offering free baby-sitting. Within four months, Angelica returned to them. And last year, they adopted Angelica, ending her bruising journey through the foster-care system.

Kids' Needs First

New federal legislation has changed the way states are supposed to handle foster care and adoption so that what is best for children is to be uppermost in the minds of case workers.

The federal Adoption and Safe Families Act (ASFA), enacted in January 1998, aims to double the number of adoptions by 2002. The new law speeds up the procedure to place foster children into adoptive families, giving states, placement agencies, and ministries strong incentives to put the needs of children first.

Although Angelica's story has an upbeat ending, the same cannot be said for many of the other 500,000 foster children in America. Historically, the foster-care system has focused on keeping families together, even if children pay the price physically and emotionally.

Foster-care adoptions are up sharply where aggressive community outreach programs have been initiated. Churches are increasingly viewed as a prized asset in that effort. Christians have cared for orphans since the first century. But the contemporary breakdown of the nation's foster-care system, burdened by bureaucracy, politics, and underfunding, has given church leaders fresh opportunities to care for foster children and to stimulate adoption in innovative ways.

"Foster parenting is more appealing when it's the responsibility of a community rather than just the two parents," says Ted Kulik, assistant director of the Institute for Children in Cambridge, Massachusetts.

While there is no conclusive research on what motivates people to care for a foster child, according to University of California at Berkeley researcher Richard Barth, it is very clear "that foster and adoptive parents have very high degrees of religiosity."

Kulik points to Child Share of Glendale, California, as an example of a small but growing number of Christian organizations working within the system. They have an enviable track record for introducing stability into troubled young lives. Two out of three

> *"Historically, the foster-care system has focused on keeping families together, even if children pay the price physically and emotionally."*

Child Share children stay with the same family until they are either reunited or adopted. The average foster child lives in four different homes.

Child Share links public and private agencies with foster and adoptive families. Some 250 congregations representing 20 denominations participate. Church members may serve with varying degrees of commitment, from baby-sitting and respite care to foster and adoptive parenting.

Nationwide, about 200,000 foster children are either presently or potentially available for adoption, though each year only about 20,000 are placed in permanent homes. Increasingly, private and public workers alike acknowledge that without community involvement the new federal law will not achieve its goal of dramatically increasing resolution of foster-care cases.

Black Church Involvement

Minority children make up 64 percent of the foster-care population and remain in care longer than any other group. African Americans have always adopted children of their own race at a higher rate than white families, according to Rita Simon of American University in Washington, D.C.

African-American churches and the state of Texas are successfully partnering in the recruitment of families for foster care and adoption. Project Hustle, a program to place hard-to-adopt children, develops teams from community groups who use their networks to find families and provide them with support.

"The use of the churches was critical because of the history of the relationship between the black church and the black community," says Helen Grape, regional placement program director for the Texas Department of Protective and Regulatory Services in Fort Worth. The response from churches is greater than from other organizations.

"Without community involvement the [Adoption and Safe Family Act] will not achieve its goal of dramatically increasing resolution of foster-care cases."

"Businesses usually must offer an incentive, such as time off or insurance, to recruit people," Grape says. "The ministers say, There is a need, so come and do it, and people will more than likely follow through."

Each community group is assigned 20 to 25 children for whom they have the responsibility to help guide through the process to, ideally, a permanent, safe home.

It is a multidimensional process that Grape helps orchestrate. "You have to forget this sequential kind of planning," Grape says. "It has to be concurrent; you have to work with the family at the same time that you identify options, support systems, judges, and court people who have to be ready to do what is necessary to free kids or get kids where they need to be."

Cooperation is essential to make the new legislation effective, Grape says. "Now, more than at any other time, public and private agencies must work together to identify families, to train together, recruit together."

A similar recruiting effort that started in Chicago has been in place since 1980. One Church, One Child is a special program designed to connect African-American families, churches, and needy kids. One Church, One Child identifies adoptive families and single parents for children in need of permanent homes and has now placed 90,000 children nationwide. The vision of One

Church, One Child was to recruit at least one African-American family or single parent per church to adopt at least one child.

Racial Tensions

Transracial adoption remains a highly sensitive issue, exposing ongoing ethnic tensions within American culture. In 1972, the National Association of Black Social Workers condemned transracial adoption as "cultural genocide." But laws enacted in 1994 and 1997 prohibit using race as a determining factor in adoption. Nevertheless, bias against transracial adoption remains.

"There is a very aggressive movement within the social services system that a black child in need of adoptive parents will not be permitted to be adopted by white couples," Fagan says. "That is their putting a race-cultural issue ahead of the actual needs of a particular child."

Critics claim that children lose their identity and become "spiritual and cultural orphans." But a 20-year study of Midwest families by Simon challenges that notion. Most parents work hard—perhaps even too hard—she says, at teaching their children about their cultural heritage.

> *"Regardless of the number of foster children available for adoption, there are still not enough adults signed up to be foster or adoptive parents."*

"The joke among these children was that not every dinner conversation has to be a discussion of black history or whether Jesse Jackson is going to run for public office," says Simon. Children were more interested in discussing basketball or dating.

As the parents of three mixed-race children, James and Karen Stobaugh of Downingtown, Pennsylvania, have more of a personal stake than most in the debate. James Stobaugh says, "At times we've struggled with our society's subtle and not-so-subtle racism." The Stobaughs relocated after racists burned crosses at a nighttime rally on the edge of their property. A firm supporter of transracial adoption, Stobaugh says, "The U.S. is home to nearly 200 people groups. To think they can or should be kept separate is totally untenable. And the people who end up paying the price are innocent children."

More Homes Needed

Regardless of the number of foster children available for adoption, there are still not enough adults signed up to be foster or adoptive parents. A common belief is that the most needy children are not adopted from foster care because adoptive white parents are interested only in healthy newborns. That is a myth, according to Conna Craig, director of the Institute for Children. She points to the Children with AIDS Project in Phoenix, which has recruited more than 1,000 parents to adopt AIDS orphans and HIV-positive babies.

Craig concedes that the longer a child is in the system, the more the likelihood of adoption dwindles. But Craig emphasizes that the notion that nobody wants older children or children with emotional and physical problems is untrue. Research indicates that no child is unadoptable, says Craig. Her organization commissioned a study by the Polling Company, which found that 71 percent of adults would, if deciding to adopt, consider a child who had spent time in foster care.

Fagan says, "We have no major national efforts going on in adoption, and there are potentially up to 2 million who would be willing to adopt if asked."

To increase adoptions, one public perception in need of change is the belief that the foster-care system is too intimidating. Don Simkovich, director of church relations for Child Share, says, "This system walks into your living room—attorney, birth parents, birth parents' attorney, judge, social workers, social worker's supervisor. It takes an adventurous spirit to work through the system."

As foster parents, Richard and Lisa Pferdner of Chatsworth, California, have placed themselves in the crossfire between parents and the state. The casualty rate for foster parents is extremely high. Many drop out within a year when they witness the painful battle over children in the system. Most important to the Pferdners now is the support their faith and Christian community provides in their demanding role as foster parents to Taylor, who came to them one year ago at the age of six months.

Even though Taylor's birth mother said from the beginning that she does not want to work toward reunification, Taylor remains in a holding pattern while the court gives a legitimate opportunity for blood relatives to seek custody.

Meanwhile, the Pferdners' dual task is to work toward family reunification even as they hold themselves out as Taylor's potential adoptive parents. Once a week they take Taylor to his birth mother, who the Pferdners say loves her son. But she has drug-related problems that make her an unreliable parent. Parental abuse of alcohol and other drugs is a factor in the placement of more than 75 percent of all children in care, according to the U.S. General Accounting Office. "It's so easy to look at the dysfunctional parents and say, 'I could give this person a better home,'" Richard Pferdner says.

Pferdner compares foster parenting to foreign missionary work. "Being a foster parent is on that level of intensity, being in the trenches in direct spiritual warfare, having your faith completely tested."

"Too many foster children are needlessly delayed in being permanently placed into adoptive families."

Under the new federal law, foster parents are being given greater powers in determining the fate of foster children in their care. Foster parents must now be notified every time the court schedules a hearing and be given the opportunity to voice their opinion on the child's status.

Child Share executive director Joanne Feldmeth believes that new legislation will take time to be applied at the local level. "It's an enormous change, and be-cause people aren't ready, because social workers have been schooled in the old line of thought that family reunification was the only way to go, it's going to take a long time for it to filter out."

Cutting the Cost of Waiting

Foster care has the reputation for being the kiss of death for an at-risk child's mental and emotional well-being.

Connecticut officials estimate that 75 percent of youths in the state's criminal justice system have been in foster care at some point in their lives. Experts say that placement in three or more foster families is the highest risk factor for a child who ultimately ends up in prison.

Studies also show that former foster-care wards make up a substantial portion of the nation's homeless. A 1991 national study found that 25 percent of foster-care wards had been homeless at some point.

Fagan says that too many foster children are needlessly delayed in being per-manently placed into adoptive families. National statistics show that the number of foster children has increased by 65 percent over the past decade. Fagan calls delay of permanent placement "child abuse by the child protective services."

Until the ASFA legislation, states had a disincentive to place children in adop-tive homes, in part because budgets were based on the number of foster chil-dren under state care. This disincentive results in children bouncing in and out of multiple foster homes, triggering many educational and emotional problems.

The ASFA plan to make foster care temporary gives federal money to each state that places more children into adoption. It aims to double—to 54,000 an-nually within the next four years—the number of children adopted out of foster care and to reduce status hearings from a maximum of 18 months to 12 months.

Substance-Abuse Treatment Must Be Made Available to Abusive Parents

by Mary Nelson

About the author: *Mary Nelson is the administrator of the Division of Adult, Children, and Family Services in the Iowa Department of Human Services. The following viewpoint is adapted from her testimony before the House Committee on Ways and Means, Subcommittee on Human Resources on March 23, 2000.*

State human service administrators and child welfare directors have identified substance abuse by parents as one of the most pervasive problems affecting the child welfare system today. The facts are staggering. An estimated 40 to 80 percent of the children who are involved with the child welfare system have families with alcohol and drug problems. In my own state of Iowa, over 50 percent of our family foster care cases involve parental substance abuse, and at least one-third of our "in-home" cases involve parental substance abuse. In Polk County, which contains our state's largest city, Des Moines, the Youth Law Center reports that 55 percent of new child welfare referrals to Juvenile Court (in-home supervision and placement cases) involve parental substance abuse.

National studies indicate that children whose parents abuse alcohol and other drugs (AOD) are almost three times likelier to be abused and more than four times likelier to be neglected than children of parents who are not substance abusers. Children from families with alcohol and drug problems are more likely to remain in out-of-home care for longer periods of time and have less chance of being reunited with their parents or adopted. They also are at greater risk of reentering care once they are returned. While the majority of these families require some kind of substance abuse service, studies suggest that less than one-third are able to be provided with treatment.

Excerpted from Mary Nelson, congressional testimony at a hearing on child protection issues, March 23, 2000.

Rethinking Current Service Delivery

These statistics point to the serious lack of alcohol and drug treatment services nationally, a problem which is compounded by a lack of appropriate and effective service interventions tailored to women with children, particularly those who come to the attention of the child welfare system. While there are good examples of treatment programs that have been effective for women and children, most substance abuse services are not designed to meet the specific needs of the child welfare population. Studies show a high failure rate for engaging and retaining in treatment women with children in foster care. More must be done to develop and increase the availability and effectiveness of such programs. A redesign and rethinking of current service delivery is critical to addressing these challenges as well as an expansion of services to address the unmet need.

The federal substance abuse confidentiality laws and its implementation add to these challenges. Confidentiality barriers, whether imposed by statute or in practice, can often prevent critical information from being shared across systems. Caseworkers cannot make critical safety and permanency decisions if they do not know how the parent is progressing in treatment or if they are attending. Judges are reluctant to reunify families or terminate parental rights if they do not have the critical information needed to make informed decisions about safety and permanency.

None of these challenges are new to child welfare directors. These issues have confronted the child welfare system from the time of the crack cocaine epidemic and have continued with the rise of methamphetamines and the resurgence of heroin. But what is new is the Adoption and Safe Families Act (ASFA) and the urgent need to achieve permanency for children in expedited timeframes.

The problems of alcohol and drug abuse among families involved with the child welfare system and the inadequacy of resources and appropriate treatment have become especially apparent since the enactment of ASFA. States are committed to ASFA's goals of safety, permanency and well being for children in the child welfare system. The need for closer connections between the child welfare system and the alcohol and drug system is clear—now more than ever. The complex issues facing their common clients call for both systems to work together to find better ways of treating families and addressing the safety, permanency and well being of children.

A Shortage of Adequate Resources

These problems transcend the availability of sufficient resources. We must do better with what we have. But the extent of these problems far outstrips the current resources of either system and additional funding, including federal funding, is needed. Funding for Title IV-B has competing service demands. The Substance Abuse Block Grant has priorities and set-asides, and there is not enough funding to meet the competing claims on those dollars from other populations such as criminal justice. Medicaid is limited in its ability to pay for the range of comprehensive services that need to be part of substance abuse treatment for parents in the child welfare system, particularly with respect to non-medical supportive services. Medicaid does cover medical treatment, such as inpatient detoxification, but does not cover a wide range of preventive and supportive services that are necessary to ensure successful outcomes. Title IV-E does not cover substance abuse services and child welfare waivers for these services have been limited to date.

Good practice demands that parents be appropriately assessed and engaged in treatment early on, unless of course, risk to the child makes reunification inappropriate. Treatment interventions must be improved to achieve measurable progress in shorter timeframes. Child welfare agencies and family court judges must have the critical information from AOD treatment providers to assess risk and safety, and make informed permanency decisions. Without the above, children will likely remain in foster care because judges will not terminate parental rights if services have not been provided, or families will be broken up when they might otherwise have remained intact with the provision of services. Initial screening and assessment, coupled with early treatment and enhanced engagement and retention strategies, will make it more likely that realistic assessments of the likelihood of reunification or appropriateness of other permanency options can be made

> *"While the majority of [abusive] families require some kind of substance abuse service, studies suggest that less than one-third are able to be provided with treatment."*

within the timetables mandated by the ASFA. The states are accountable and committed to meeting these new timetables. However, increased resources are essential to improving the capacity of states to meet the ASFA mandates.

National Partnerships

With the enactment of the ASFA in November 1997, American Public Human Services Association (APHSA) and The National Association of State Alcohol and Drug Abuse Directors (NASADAD) members felt it was imperative to bring state agencies from both systems—child welfare and AOD—to the table as problem solvers. Our associations formed a task force in March of 1998 to work together, with the goal of improving the accessibility and effectiveness of appropriate substance abuse prevention and treatment services for families in the child abuse and neglect and foster care systems. APHSA and NASADAD identified the following issues for joint attention by its members and the workgroup:

- Developing shared knowledge and understanding on the part of both systems regarding underlying values and missions of each system, as well as identifying ways to work more collaboratively across systems.
- Developing shared knowledge and understanding on the part of both sys-

tems of the impact of AOD issues on families in the child welfare system.
- Need for and development of shared screening tools, training for child welfare (e.g., on assessing need for AOD treatment) and AOD staff (e.g., on risk assessment and permanency planning), joint protocols for collaborative work at the practice level, data collection and performance measures.
- Identifying and developing methods for better engaging families referred by child welfare into AOD treatment, keeping them engaged in treatment, and re-engaging them when necessary; as well as identifying and developing treatment methods that can achieve success with families in shorter time frames.
- Identifying and developing ways to work within existing federal laws, as well as changes in federal laws which may serve as barriers to working together (e.g., confidentiality prohibitions, which may limit cooperation and coordination).
- Identifying and disseminating information about successful models of joint child welfare and AOD programs.
- Addressing the need for additional resources for prevention, treatment, and other essential support services; and ways to access and utilize various federal, state and local funding streams.

APHSA and NASADAD also developed joint recommendations in response to the Department of Health and Human Services (HHS) Report to Congress required by ASFA entitled Blending Perspectives and Building Common Ground. APHSA and NASADAD urged HHS to provide leadership and support for a variety of activities including improving and expanding treatment and services, improving state systems and collaboration, identification and dissemination of best practices, support for state-based cross training, addressing confidentiality barriers, increasing federal funding for prevention, treatment and aftercare, and removal of barriers to current funding streams to make them work more effectively, and enhancing research, data and performance. The ultimate goal is to develop, enhance and sustain an array of comprehensive and timely services including prevention and early intervention that addresses the needs of children and families in the child welfare system. . . .

In March 2000, APHSA's policy-making body, the National Council of State Human Service Administrators, adopted a policy resolution to address the serious problem of substance abuse and its impact on children and families in the child welfare system. The council's policy asks Congress to consider the creation of a child welfare and substance abuse initiative to enhance state agency capacity to collaborate on the development of a comprehensive system of services to address the prevention and treatment needs of families with substance abuse problems who come into contact with the child welfare system. Such an initiative should be developed in consultation with the states. We support additional federal funding for this critical area, however, we must emphasize that new federal funding for this initiative should not come at the expense of other human service programs. In addition, the resolution urges Congress to maintain core funding for current critical public human service programs. . . .

Information sharing among substance abuse, child welfare agencies and the courts is critical to making permanency and safety decisions for children and to achieving positive service outcomes. APHSA is committed to examining the barriers that federal confidentiality statute and regulations pose to states, educating key stakeholders on these issues, and to recommending statutory, regulatory and/or practice changes that would better facilitate sharing and disclosure of information between the two systems. We believe sharing of information is especially critical

> *"The need for closer connections between the child welfare system and the alcohol and drug system is clear."*

around assessing progress in treatment, assuring safety and making informed decisions regarding permanency.

Furthermore, APHSA urges Congress and the Administration, to the fullest extent possible, to increase the flexibility of IV-E, Medicaid and the Substance Abuse Prevention and Treatment Block Grant. Increased flexibility would enable funding to be used to provide a variety of substance abuse treatment and prevention services to the families who come into contact with the child welfare system.

We believe that realization of these recommendations will provide states with the needed resources and capacity to promote safety, permanency, well being and parental recovery in families who come to the attention of the child welfare system.

Chapter 4

Will Changes in the Criminal Justice System Help Prevent Child Sexual Abuse?

Preventing Child Sexual Abuse: An Overview

by Sarah Glazer

About the author: *Sarah Glazer is a freelance writer in New York who specializes in health care and social policy issues.*

Shortly before convicted child molester Earl Shriner was scheduled to be released from a Washington state prison in 1988, prison officials faced an awful dilemma. They knew Shriner had drawn pictures and written in his diary about torturing children once he was free, but he had served his sentence and had to be released. Prison officials tried to have Shriner committed to a mental institution, but a judge ruled that he was not mentally ill under the law.

Five months after his release, Shriner raped and sexually mutilated a 7-year-old boy.

The case raised an outcry in Washington state and led to the passage of a comprehensive legislative package aimed at stopping another Earl Shriner. One statute permits police to notify residents when a recently released sex offender moves into the neighborhood. Another permits the state to hold "sexually violent predators" indefinitely in a mental-treatment wing of the state prison.

Since then, dozens of states have passed similarly tough statutes, often following horrifying sexual crimes in their own backyards. As of December 1995, 30 states had passed community-notification laws.

Civil Liberties Concerns

But the laws have been challenged by civil libertarians as attacks on the rights of prisoners who have served the full sentence for their crimes. In New Jersey, a federal judge has declared the state's notification law unconstitutional, saying it amounts to a second punishment on offenders who committed their crimes before the law took effect January 1, 1995.

Laws that permit dangerous sexual predators to be detained beyond their sentences have been challenged in five states—Washington, Wisconsin, Kansas, Minnesota and Iowa. Minnesota passed its statute in 1994, joining a growing

Excerpted from Sarah Glazer, "Punishing Sex Offenders," *CQ Researcher*, January 12, 1996. Reprinted with permission from *CQ Researcher*.

number of states that detain sex offenders with mental disorders who are "likely to engage" in future sexual crimes. The law was prompted by the scheduled release of 54-year-old Dennis Linehan, a rapist and murderer. Linehan is challenging the law as unconstitutional.

"It's a long stretch from our system of due process and the standard of proof beyond a reasonable doubt to this prediction of future dangerousness," says attorney Kathleen Milner of the Minnesota Civil Liberties Union, which filed an amicus brief on behalf of Linehan. "Conceivably, after sex offenders they'll move on to other areas: 'Well, you're likely to shoplift again, so we're going to hold you.'"

Crime or Mental Illness?

The tough anti-predator laws raise basic questions about how sex offenses should be viewed: Are they caused by mental illnesses that can be treated with therapy? Or are they crimes, plain and simple, that should be punished?

The mental health profession is divided over the issue. And there is vigorous debate over which, if any, treatments are effective in rehabilitating sex offenders.

The Washington State Psychiatric Association is among those challenging the state's sexual predator law, under which the state currently is holding 32 sex offenders beyond their sentences. "These are merely criminals," says Seattle psychiatrist James D. Reardon, an association spokesman. "There is no scientifically based effective treatment for sex offenders. We couldn't find any research [showing] that treating is any more effective than incarcerating."

But some experts who work with sex offenders insist they have found therapies that work, among them Fred S. Berlin, director of the National Institute for the Study, Prevention and Treatment of Sexual Trauma in Baltimore, Md. "I don't think the majority [of sex offenders] have a condition that's curable," he says, "but I do think that many of them have a psychiatric disorder and can, like alcoholics, learn to control themselves and live safely in the community."

"There are probably sex offenders who are criminals and some who are mentally ill," says Roxanne Lieb, associate director of the Washington State Institute for Public Policy at Evergreen State College in Olympia, WA. It's not black and white, as it's been posed in this debate." Certain therapies may help specific types of sex offenders but have little effect on others who are more likely to reoffend, Lieb says.

"[Minnesota joined] a growing number of states that detain sex offenders with mental disorders who are 'likely to engage' in future sexual crimes."

"Incest offenders are in a very different category from a compulsive pedophile who targets little boys, has done it 20 times and will do it 20 times more," says Lieb. "With an incest offender violating his daughter, it's not sexual drive; it's more typically issues of power and control." Incest offenders—usually fathers, stepfathers and uncles—are also the least likely of all sex offenders to commit sex crimes again—particularly outside the family.

The most well-publicized cases tend to focus on violence by strangers. Yet rape-murders constitute fewer than 3 percent of all sex offenses, and sadistic sex offenders are equally uncommon, according to Robert E. Freeman-Longo of the Safer Society Foundation in Brandon, VT, which tracks sex-offender treatment programs nationwide and provides treatment referral.

"Some experts who work with sex offenders insist they have found therapies that work."

In almost 90 percent of the molestation cases leading to convictions, the children know their abuser, according to the federal Bureau of Justice Statistics (BJS). In almost half the cases, the abuser is a parent or relative. Similarly, adults are more likely to be raped by someone they know than by strangers; acquaintances, boyfriends or family members represent about 60 percent of convicted rapists.

"The public always hates the sex offenders it doesn't know and believes they should all go to prison forever," says Lucy Berliner, research director at the Harborview Sexual Assault Center in Seattle, which treats assault victims. "The one they do know—their brother, their son, their pastor—they want to have the opportunity to get rehabilitated."

Berliner served on the task force that drafted Washington state's pioneering sex predator law. She defends the law against assaults by civil libertarians, arguing that it's narrowly drawn to get at a few hard-core, repetitive offenders like Shriner.

Balancing Rights

For policy-makers, it comes down to a balancing act between the rights of ex-offenders and the rights of potential victims. "Is the state helpless?" asks Alexander D. Brooks, professor of law emeritus at Rutgers Law School in Newark, NJ. "Must the state release such a person and say it can't do anything until he commits another crime?"

Initially, Brooks expected to oppose the Washington state law on civil liberties grounds, but he changed his mind after contemplating the legal impasse Washington state faced in the Shriner case.

"Which interest are you more concerned about protecting?" he asks. "Keeping dangerous offenders on the street, where they will commit sexual offenses against women and children, or protecting women and children by committing the most dangerous offenders with the hope of treating them?"

As courts and legislatures debate how to deal with sex offenders, here are some of the questions being asked:

Should citizens be informed of sex offenders living in their community?

In July 1994, in a suburb of Trenton, NJ, 7-year-old Megan Kanka walked across the street to see a neighbor's puppy. She never came home. Jesse Timmendequas, a neighbor and twice-convicted sex offender, has been charged with murdering Megan. Jury selection in his long-delayed trial is set to begin in February [1996].

Unbeknown to the neighborhood, Timmendequas had spent six years in Avenel, New Jersey's treatment-prison for sex offenders, for molesting and attempting to kill another little girl.

Within weeks of Megan's death, more than 200,000 New Jerseyans had signed a petition demanding that government officials notify communities when sex offenders move into the neighborhood.

In October 1994, Republican Gov. Christine Todd Whitman signed a package of 10 bills, which came to be called "Megan's Law." The most controversial provision requires released sex offenders to register with local police.

In addition, neighborhoods must be told the identity, criminal record and address of sex offenders who prosecutors think pose a high risk of reoffending. If the risk is low, only law enforcement officers are notified. If the risk is moderate, organizations such as schools and day-care organizations are notified. If the risk is high, all residents of the offender's neighborhood must be notified through such methods as distributing handbills or door-to-door visits.

Encouraging Vigilantism?

Although New Jersey has had relatively little experience with the law so far, there already have been some problems with it, according to Edward Martone, executive director of the American Civil Liberties Union of New Jersey.

Shortly after the law took effect in January 1995, a father and son in Phillipsburg, NJ, broke into a house where a recently paroled sex offender was living. They beat up a man sleeping on the couch whom they mistook for the parolee.

Vigilantism is one of the major arguments that has been raised against notification laws. In Washington state, which in 1990 became the first state to approve notification, a sex offender's house was burned down after his community was notified. In the law's first three years, there were approximately 14 incidents against sex offenders ranging from insults to rock-throwing, according to the Institute for Public Policy.

> *"For policy-makers, it comes down to a balancing act between the rights of ex-offenders and the rights of potential victims."*

The law's advocates respond that the vigilantism has been minimal considering that communities were notified about 176 sex offenders during the period. Berliner also points out that before the law the public often learned of neighbors charged with repellent crimes through weekly records of arrests printed in local newspapers.

Catherine Broderick, who heads a unit in the Morris County, NJ, prosecutors office responsible for implementing Megan's Law, says that each notification her office makes will include a warning that vigilante activities will be prosecuted. Broderick notes that the Phillipsburg men who mistakenly attacked a neighbor have been prosecuted. "The idea is not to punish people further for offenses," she says. "The idea is to educate the public as a tool to prevent future victims."

Will They Work?

But critics doubt the laws will work. They point to a recent study in Washington state which found no difference in rearrest rates among sex offenders since passage of the community notification law five years ago.

In Camden County, NJ, a sex offender whose community had been notified raped a child at a fast-food restaurant in a neighboring town. The incident shows the bill "is an incentive to get out of town, to hide," Martone says. "It's cruelly ironic that the notification bill is causing people to seek anonymity. It's the worst way to deal with repetitive and compulsive sex offenders. It gives them reason to avoid family, treatment, detection and take it on the lam."

> *"Advance publicity won't necessarily deter sex offenders within their own neighborhood."*

Advance publicity won't necessarily deter sex offenders within their own neighborhood, either, Martone adds. He cites the recent case of a 15-year-old Lakewood, NJ, boy who was raped in the apartment of a released sex offender despite warnings about the man sent to area residents, including the boy's parents. The law, Martone asserts, "doesn't provide protection. It says, 'Here's a picture of a guy we think is a time bomb. Have a nice day.'"

Freeman-Longo at the Safer Society Foundation also opposes notification laws. In New Jersey, some incest victims now fear reporting their abuse because of the public humiliation that could be created by the public notification law, he said in a recent report. "If notification prevails, how fair is it for a child to go to school and hear others talk about his or her brother, father or grandfather, the sexual offender?"

"We know low self-esteem and lack of an ingrained social structure are factors that feed into [abusive] behavior," he says. "Public notification will worsen some of the problems."

Broderick concedes that the notification laws "will not eliminate child abuse." She admits, "Quite frankly, for this really to work, it would have to become a national program." But she says notification still provides a sense of relief to parents and has educated families to the dangers of sexual abuse.

When Broderick has knocked on doors to inform residents that a sex offender is living in their neighborhood, she says there's usually a double reaction—shock followed by calm. "The second reaction is a kind of confidence. 'At least

I know this and can work with my child and any other member of the family that needs to know.'"

Alerting neighbors means some sex offenders are caught earlier in the cycle of recidivism. In Washington state, offenders identified by community notification were arrested for new crimes much earlier than similar offenders released before the notification law—a median of about two years vs. five years for the comparison group.

> *"Alerting neighbors means some sex offenders are caught earlier in the cycle of recidivism."*

Often, the rearrests are for more minor charges, such as communicating with a minor for immoral purposes, according to Lieb of the Institute for Public Policy, which conducted the study. Detectives in some counties have been assigned to offenders targeted by community notification and may be giving them intensified scrutiny, she suggests.

Berliner says the law was drafted not so much to reduce crime but in response to citizens who say they have a right to be informed. "If a person who has raped and molested numerous children . . . moves in next-door and you have young children, do you want to know about it?" Berliner asks. "Citizens do."

Civil Commitment

Should sex offenders be kept in confinement after they have served their prison sentences?

Washington state changed the nation's legal landscape in 1990 when it broadened its laws confining sexual criminals once their prison sentences had expired. Traditionally, Washington and other states permitted the involuntary hospitalization of mentally ill persons considered dangerous through civil commitment procedures. Washington's law was so narrowly drawn that convicted molester Shriner could not be detained after completing his sentence.

But the 1990 law targeted a new class of offender, the "sexually violent predator." The law defined a predator as someone charged with or convicted of a crime of sexual violence who suffers from a "mental abnormality or personality disorder" which makes the person likely to commit future predatory sexual acts. Offenders deemed by a court to fit that definition can be confined at a prison treatment facility indefinitely—until considered safe to be released into the community.

A federal judge has declared such confinement unconstitutional because it punishes the same crime twice. In an opinion issued Aug. 25, 1995, John C. Coughenour, a U.S. District Judge in Seattle, called the law "an unconstitutional second punishment," violating the Constitution's ex post facto and double jeopardy clauses as well as the offender's due-process rights.

The state of Washington has appealed the decision and is expected to take it to the Supreme Court if necessary.

Because Shriner had told a cellmate about his plans to attack small children on his release, prison officials sought to commit him to a mental hospital under Washington's law for sexual psychopaths. But a judge turned down their request. Shriner did not fit the definition of a mentally ill person under the narrowly drawn statute and had not committed a recent overt act proving he was dangerous.

"Generally, the interpretation of [the psychopath law] is they are psychotic and out of touch with reality," Berliner explains, "so our [predator] bill and the ones adopted in the states since then have used a different definition of what is wrong with these people."

Washington's new legislation was intended "to fill the gap in our sentencing structure to cover people who have completed their sentences and are still dangerous" but may not be crazy under a strict definition, Berliner says. There are "people in prison fantasizing about going out and raping and killing children. Well, people [in Washington state] said, 'We don't accept that there's nothing you can do about that situation.'"

Berliner argues that the new law, which has become a model for several other states, was narrowly drawn, thus limiting the impact on most prisoners' civil liberties. In fact, only 32 offenders, less than 1 percent of all imprisoned sex offenders in the state, have been confined under the new statute.

"Pseudo-Mental Definition"

But the law's opponents contend that the state is detaining sex offenders who aren't mentally ill under the guise of mental health treatment. "You can't put someone who is not mentally ill in an institution," says Robert C. Boruchowitz, an attorney in the Seattle Public Defender's office who represents eight of the 32 offenders. "And the state is basically pretending our guys are mentally ill to get around the due-process problem."

One of Boruchowitz's clients is Andre Brigham Young, a three-time convicted rapist, who has challenged his commitment under the predator statute as unconstitutional. His case will be heard before the Ninth Circuit Court of Appeals.

> *"You can't put someone who is not mentally ill in an institution."*

Boruchowitz argues that the Legislature was trying to find a "pseudo-mental definition" to get around the rights of released prisoners. "Mental abnormality" is not a clinically recognized term, he notes. And the term "personality disorder," which generally refers to a person's history of maladaptive behavior, is so broad that it encompasses "virtually everyone in prison," he argues.

Psychiatrist Reardon agrees. "These people deliberately decide to commit a crime. To say illness causes them to commit a crime is ridiculous." Though Reardon agrees the behavior is abnormal and may even be compulsive, he asserts, "to say someone who has this compulsion is mentally ill is stretching the boundaries of mental illness."

Reardon also views the treatment offered in prison as essentially a sham. "All the surveys show there is no treatment being done. The [staff] are not trained. The program is not organized."

Boruchowitz says his clients feel more like prisoners in the mental wing than they did behind conventional bars. "It's a maximum security facility," he says. "There's barbed wire all around it. The guards are instructed to shoot anyone who tries to escape."

In a highly critical 1992 evaluation of the treatment program, Canadian psychologist Vernon L. Quinsey noted that offenders being held were "embittered" by the additional confinement and that only three were actively engaged in treatment. He also pointed out an apparent contradiction in the new law. The statute is directed at those offenders unlikely to be "cured," yet it requires them to receive treatment—with their release conditional on a court or jury decision that they are no longer a threat.

The program's lack of any procedure for releasing offenders on a gradual or temporary basis into the community is a "fatal problem," Quinsey concluded. Without it, staff had only the offender's behavior in the "artificial" environment of the prison on which to base predictions of future dangerousness.

Four years later, the state still has not introduced a gradual-release program for these specially designated sex offenders, Boruchowitz says, and not a single offender has been declared safe enough by staff to be released permanently.

"There is no question there have been problems," Berliner concedes. But she argues the treatment program could be improved in the future and that new treatments may be developed to render this class of sex offenders less dangerous. "The law shouldn't be found unconstitutional because it's a crummy treatment program," she argues.

A Dangerous Precedent?

But civil libertarians say the law sets a dangerous precedent for detaining other kinds of lawbreakers on the basis of what they might do in the future. Eric S. Janus, a professor at William Mitchell College of Law in St. Paul, MN, says a Minnesota law modeled on Washington's statute "is pure preventive detention." Potentially, warns Janus, "The principle underlying it would swallow the entire criminal justice system."

Janus is one of the attorneys representing rapist-murderer Linehan, who at age 24 strangled a 14-year-old babysitter who resisted his advances. Trial testimony revealed that in addition to the babysitter, Linehan assaulted several women before being caught and imprisoned. In 1975, Linehan escaped from prison and fled to Michigan, where he was imprisoned for assaulting a 12-year-old girl. In 1983, at the completion of his Michigan sentence, he was returned to Minnesota and incarcerated.

On May 15, 1992, Linehan was scheduled to be released. Instead, he was committed to a state mental hospital under Minnesota's "psychopathic personality" law. However, the state Supreme Court overturned Linehan's commitment in June 1994, saying he did not fit the law's definition of a psychopath as someone unable to control his sexual impulses.

Under a new law, passed in August 1994 in response to Linehan's imminent release, prosecutors need only prove that someone is unwilling to control his or her sexual impulses. The new statute permits the commitment of "sexually dangerous persons" who have a history of past harmful sexual conduct, are likely to repeat the conduct in the future and have a personality disorder.

Linehan was committed under the new law, which he challenged on constitutional grounds. In July 1995, a district judge upheld Linehan's indefinite commitment, saying, "Commitment is necessary for the protection of the public." But the real test will come in the appellate courts. Meanwhile, Linehan remains in a state mental hospital.

"One of the reasons we think this law is so destructive is it puts therapists and courts in the position of gazing into a very cloudy crystal ball and predicting the future," says Janus. He describes Linehan, who has spent 27 years in prison, as "no different from any other criminal."

"What could Linehan do to show he's not dangerous?" Janus asks. "He's had 20 years of good behavior [in prison] and that's not good enough. He's gone through treatment and that's not enough."

Some psychologists say they've developed good instruments for predicting who is dangerous. Quinsey has developed a prediction tool, based largely on the offender's past history, which is "as good or slightly better than short-term weather forecasting," predicting accurately in 75 percent of cases, he says.

But that confidence is by no means unanimously shared in the field. "You can flip a coin and get a better prediction than by clinical evaluation," Reardon maintains.

Community Notification Laws Protect Children from Child Molesters

by Dan Lungren

About the author: *Dan Lungren is a former California attorney general.*

In the [San Francisco] Bay Area, a father viewing the CD-ROM confirmed that his ex-wife's boyfriend, with whom she lives, is a registered sex offender.

In less than one month's time, the Megan's Law CD-ROM directory of nearly 64,000 California sex offenders has proved its greatest worth: protecting children from the horror of molestation.

Molesters have been caught. Sex offenders who refused to properly register with police have been located and arrested. Mothers have been alerted that men near their kids—even boyfriends, in some cases—are sex offenders. All this because California has finally lifted the cloak of anonymity that has shielded sex offenders from public view for decades.

Megan's Law Produces Dramatic Results

But you might not know that from reading some newspapers. While we have seen front-page drama about the difficult implementation of Megan's Law, stories such as these have been given short shrift:

• A Sacramento County woman viewed the CD-ROM and noticed the photo of a man who regularly spent time playing with children, including her own, at a community swimming pool. She notified other parents, one of whom then contacted the sheriff's department. Sheriff's investigators found that the sex offender was not living at his registered address and was actually living with a woman and her three children—a violation of his probation. He was arrested and now stands accused of molesting a 13-year-old girl at that residence.

• In the Bay Area, a father viewing the CD-ROM confirmed that his ex-wife's boyfriend, with whom she lives, is a registered sex offender. The in-

Reprinted from Dan Lungren, "Shining New Light on Sex Offenders: How Megan's Law Is Working for Californians," *San Diego Union-Tribune*, July 31, 1997. Reprinted with permission from the author.

quiring father's two young daughters also live with his ex-wife. She was unaware of her live-in boyfriend's conviction for child molestation. The father obtained a restraining order, barring the sex offender from any further contact with his daughters.

• A San Diego grandmother, suspecting that her former daughter-in-law and mother of her four grandchildren had remarried a convicted sex offender, waited anxiously to check the database the first day it was available. "I said, 'what if he's a rapist?' and sure as hell, he was," the grandmother told the Associated Press. She said she planned to use the information to wage a visitation battle with the mother over the three girls and one boy, all under age 10.

Outdated Information?

While many newspaper accounts have reported—justifiably—that some sex offender information in the Megan's Law CD-ROM is outdated, that isn't even half the story. In fact, the names of the sex offenders identified on the CD-ROM, and their recorded sex offenses, are accurate. Sex-offender identities are the most important data, as the incidents above prove.

So what part of the CD-ROM is outdated? Mostly, the news media have reported that the residence zip code data is outdated for as many as 40 percent of the sex offenders in the database. However, law enforcement openly said that from the outset. Tracking sex offenders who refuse to properly register with police has always been difficult. One reason is that a convicted sex offender who wants to keep police in the dark about his whereabouts will refuse to accurately register his location—even though it means breaking the law.

Just a few years ago, as many as 70 percent or 80 percent of convicted sex offenders had not properly registered. Since it was only a misdemeanor offense, there was little for the sex offender to fear. But we've started turning that problem around in three ways: First, we toughened the penalty for failing to register—it can now be charged as a felony.

Second, we enacted three-strikes laws, meaning prosecutors can often charge that felony as a second or third strike and put the sex offender in prison for a much longer sentence. Third, we launched an unprecedented state effort in cooperation with local law enforcement to track down "underground" sex offenders.

> *"In less than one month's time, the Megan's Law CD-ROM directory . . . has proved its greatest worth: protecting children from the horror of molestation."*

Our state Sexual Predator Apprehension Teams are highly trained units, dedicated solely to locating and, wherever appropriate, arresting these dangerous individuals. Not surprisingly, thousands more sex offenders have decided to properly register with police in the last few years. Now, with the Megan's Law CD-ROM, law enforcement has the eyes and ears of law-abiding people involved in this effort. Most sex offenders, fearful of the greater likelihood of being found and longer prison sentences, will choose to accurately register with police.

Violent and Repeat Offenders

Still, we cannot kid ourselves. Some sex offenders—particularly among the 1,600 high-risk sex offenders who have committed multiple and/or violent sex crimes—will opt to dodge the authorities, no matter how tough or lenient the law. They are the most dangerous of all sex offenders, and they are perhaps the best reason for Megan's Law.

If, because of their deliberate failure to register, we do not know where some high-risk sex offenders are, we do know who they are and we know what they have done to others. All citizens should be able to share in that knowledge to protect themselves and their families, even as law enforcement goes to greater lengths to locate and, where appropriate, arrest these criminals.

"Before Megan's Law, we kept sex offenders virtually anonymous to everyone but the police."

In the end, Californians should be relieved that at long last we have reformed our sex-offender laws. Before Megan's Law, we kept sex offenders virtually anonymous to everyone but the police, who in turn were prohibited from making even the most limited disclosure about them. The old laws, for example, made it illegal for police to even warn parents living near a park that a registered sex offender had been seen lurking there. The real crime was keeping that information from parents. Megan's Law sets things right.

While they work overtime to cast doubt on Megan's Law, pundits and journalists should not forget what most of us know instinctively: If there is a question about publicly identifying sex offenders, the benefit of the doubt should go to those who merely want to protect themselves and their families from sexual assaults, not to those who have committed these vile crimes.

Civil Commitment Laws Will Reduce Child Sex Abuse

by Joe Diamond

About the author: *Joe Diamond is the public affairs director for the Center for the Community Interest, a national organization that serves as a voice for the community on crime and quality-of-life issues.*

In June 1997, the U.S. Supreme Court upheld a Kansas law allowing the state to confine sexual offenders to mental hospitals after they are released from prison. The case involved Leroy Hendricks, a 62-year-old pedophile who once told authorities that the only way he could stop molesting children was "to die." ABC News got an unintentionally hilarious quote from Hendricks' lawyer, who said his client was "shocked" by the ruling: "He and the other inmates [at the Kansas State Mental Health Correctional Facility] had gotten their hopes up and were extremely disappointed by the ruling," the attorney said.

Opening the Door for Further Protection

The disappointment of a few pedophiles is a small price to pay for the victory that the Court has given society. With Kansas' Sexual Predator Law validated, states now have considerable leeway in protecting people from deviants. Vigorous enforcement of similar laws might have saved the lives of Megan Kanka [paroled child molester Jesse Timmendequas raped and murdered Megan Kanka in July of 1994], Polly Klaas [in October of 1993, Polly Klaas was abducted and murdered by Richard Allen Davis] and countless other young victims. We can't bring back the dead, but at least we now have enhanced legal tools to prevent fresh tragedies.

Only a handful of states have similar laws, but more are expected to follow. The Center for the Community Interest (CCI), which filed a "friend of the court brief" supporting the Kansas law, is calling for revamped sex-predator laws in other

Reprinted from Joe Diamond, "Victory for Victims' Rights in Kansas," July 3, 1997, available at www.intellectualcapital.com/issues/issue95/iten2415/asp. Reprinted with permission from the author.

states. Dennis Saffran, CCI's New York regional director, says, "It's important that other states pass these laws so we can protect children like Megan Kanka from killers like Jesse Timmendequas." In New York, CCI is proposing a two-pronged bill allowing for civil commitment of dangerously deranged sex offenders, and lifetime parole supervision for sex offenders released back onto the streets.

The Fallacy of the "Slippery-Slope" Argument

It's no surprise that the American Civil Liberties Union (ACLU) (which submitted a brief opposing the Kansas law) and other criminal-rights groups are unhappy about this trend toward greater control of criminals (and less regard for their "rights"). Advocates for the deviants should be concerned about the Court's ruling, not to mention their own declining influence over the justice system. Decent people, though, have much to celebrate. And little to fear. Under the Kansas law, before confining sex offenders to an institution the state must prove both that the detainee is dangerous, and that he has a mental abnormality or personality disorder rendering him unable to control his criminal behavior. How many law-abiding citizens fit even one of those criteria, let alone all of them?

> *"In the abstract, infringing on the liberties of law-breakers may threaten 'everyone.' But in the real world, it actually saves lives."*

The *New York Times*, in its pretentious way, wrote an editorial denouncing the ruling: "Everyone can agree that society has a duty to protect children from violent sex offenders, but the Supreme Court has gone down a potentially dangerous road for civil liberties. . . ."

Like the ACLU, the *Times* often tries hard to portray new legal intrusions on criminals as evidence of the dreaded "slippery slope" to a police state where everyone's freedom is at stake. For most people, though, the greater threat comes not from the state, but from violent felons. In the abstract, infringing on the liberties of law-breakers may threaten "everyone." But in the real world, it actually saves lives.

The slippery-slope argument is also weak because it equates cracking down on felons (which most Americans enthusiastically support) with suppression of law-abiding people. Just because the public cheers Megan's Law doesn't mean it will sit idly by while the government strips away its freedom of speech or religion. Even the ACLU admits that politicians who enact these tougher laws are doing it to court votes. Taking away widely cherished rights isn't popular, and it's definitely not a vote-getter.

Making the Distinction Between Right and Wrong

On the other hand, notions such as due process and search-and-seizure protections have been so perverted by the criminal-rights lobby that they are almost thought of as weapons for the guilty to be used against the public.

In one sense, however, the criminal-rights lobby may have a point. America may be on its way to creating a special class of citizens that exists outside the framework of the Constitution. The Court's ruling in *Kansas v. Hendricks* is merely the latest encroachment of the state upon the lives of convicted criminals. But unlike the paranoid rantings of the ACLU, this doesn't mean we are becoming a totalitarian society. If anything, it means we are returning to the days before the Warren Court, when society drew clear lines between right and wrong.

The Supreme Court's decision to uphold Kansas' Sexually Violent Predator Act takes us further along that road. The ruling is a milestone for America in general, and the victims' rights movement in particular.

Child Molesters
Should Be Castrated

Part I: by Larry Don McQuay, Part II: by Fred S. Berlin

About the authors: *Larry Don McQuay is a convicted child molester who was paroled from prison in April 1996. In June 1997 he was convicted on another count of child molestation and sentenced to twenty years in prison. Fred S. Berlin is an associate professor at the Johns Hopkins University School of Medicine, and director of the National Institute for the Study, Prevention and Treatment of Sexual Trauma.*

I

Childrens' nightmares are haunted by demons, some imagined, others real. I'm one of the real ones; I haunt the dreams of scores of children. You'll find me in a Texas prison serving an eight year sentence for molesting a single boy. That's all the court convicted me of, but I have abused close to 200 children.

In the United States, thousands of kids meet monsters like me each year. We prowl your communities, stalking, pouncing when possible, forcing children to endure degrading, violent acts. We wear the innocent-looking masks of a father, step-father, uncle, cousin. We could wear the caring face of a baby-sitter, or a teacher, or a priest. I myself have worn various masks: brother, cousin, step-father, uncle, school-bus driver, family friend. All to molest unsuspecting boys and girls.

Scarcely a week goes by without another disturbing news report about another poor soul victimized by a child rapist. Listen carefully to that next report. Odds are that you'll hear that this same sex offender had a past conviction for molesting at least one other child.

That's because prison is not a deterrent for most sex offenders, and it definitely will not be a deterrent for me. I do not want to return to prison; I would like to be a law abiding citizen. But the threat of being incarcerated for the rest of my life—and the threat of spending, as I believe I will, an eternity in hell—will not stop me from re-offending when I am released.

Prison's Effect on Child Molesters

In fact, in many cases, prison intensifies sex offenders' conditions by making us more savage. Where once we would "playfully" undress a victim, we now roughly strip them. What was once inappropriate touching and "caressing" escalates to a full-scale invasion. What was fondling and masturbation becomes dehumanizing sodomy. What used to be a cultivated "relationship" that took time and preparation becomes an unplanned kidnapping and rape where children are beaten, tortured, ravaged, and often found dead and mutilated, or never found at all. You see, sex offenders who've been to prison not only emerge with an appetite for violence but also learn a lesson about how to stay out of jail: make sure that the next victim can't ever report them.

I speak from experience. Lately, many of my dreams and fantasies have become more violent. My sleep is plagued with fantasies of raping kidnapped children in a way that renders them unable to identify me. Without the right treatment, I believe that eventually I will rape, then murder, my victims to keep them from reporting me. That scares me. It should scare you, too.

To reduce these crimes against your children, Texas Governor Ann Richards, for example, advocates more prisons and "harsher" sentences for sex offenders, especially repeat child molesters. Thus she's pushing for more of a solution that does not work, a solution that only means I will take up bed space in one of the many new

> *"Prison is not a deterrent for most sex offenders."*

prisons she is spending millions of dollars on so that later I can commit the same crime. The fact is, prison is nothing more than an oversized, overpriced homeless shelter. Inmates are well fed and clothed and have warm beds to sleep in, all for free. To sex offenders, loss of freedom simply means there are no children available to rape. But we can get child pornography, we can fantasize about the children we watch on television, and we have the memories of our past crimes. Moreover, sex is plentiful in prison. We substitute young-looking partners for children and let our imagination do the rest.

Our victims, meanwhile, retain the searing, ghastly memories of abuse, memories that can last a lifetime. Who is punished more?

A Tragic Cycle

According to Texas statutes, as well as those of most other states, child molesters currently in prison can be paroled. But a grotesquely high percentage of all untreated sex offenders rape again. Returning us to prison makes us stop—but getting us back in jail means that another child must first fall prey. The system returns a child molester to prison after he is captured by the police, after the child-victim has suffered the torture and savagery of being abused, after the child-victim has endured a grueling and humiliating interrogation by strangers.

Always after, and always too late to save the child. Our justice system, by releasing criminals like me into communities without effective treatment, now dooms countless children to abuse. And most child rapists get away with raping many children, some over and over before being caught.

There is a civilized alternative to this tragic cycle: castrate repeat sex offenders.

Now, some good and decent citizens claim that castration itself is barbaric. What is barbaric is what I have done to so many children; refusing to castrate me is barbaric to the children I will molest. Mandatory castration of sex offenders, whether for their first, second, or third conviction of a sex offense, is currently a violation of the United States Constitution because it is considered "cruel and unusual punishment." But no punishment is crueler or more unusual than the pain I have caused my victims. Voluntary castration is not unconstitutional, but no state allows it.

> *"Our justice system, by releasing criminals like me into communities without effective treatment, now dooms countless children to abuse."*

The governor of Texas, as well as many other state governors, is well aware of the statistics and other information regarding castration, but she turns a deaf ear to my pleas. In doing so, she turns a deaf ear to the children who are my future victims. Criminals who want to be rehabilitated are rare, so it is inconceivable to me that those who volunteer to be castrated are denied this treatment.

I do not write as a scared or worried parent. I have—thankfully—no children at all. I am scared for your children. When they have nightmares, let them be about the ghouls they see in horror movies or on the Saturday morning cartoons. They shouldn't have to have nightmares about me.

My next parole date is June 1995.

II

Larry Don McQuay was once a child himself. From the innocence of youth, no doubt filled with the promise of life, he became an uncle, step-father, school bus driver, and child molester. A self-proclaimed monster who haunts the nightmares of children, fearful himself of spending eternity in hell, who is Mr. McQuay and what should we do with him?

To be sure, even the mention of castration has an ugly, jarring sound to it; it is an idea that polite people naturally shrink from. But as Mr. McQuay's own words show, there is a terrible problem out there and the ways we are currently trying to solve it aren't working. So if castration, in any form and even in combination with other measures such as counseling, strikes you as the wrong solution, keep thinking about the problem, because everyone can agree that putting people like Mr. McQuay back on the streets is crazy.

Let's be clear about the stakes here. According to the U.S. Department of

Health and Human Services, approximately two out of every 1,000 children have been sexually abused, a figure that totaled 138,000 youngsters nationally in 1986. A significant percentage of this figure likely reflects the prevalence of pedophilia in a given community. Because of the driven nature of the disorder, an individual pedophile may make contact with 2 or 3 different children per week, some of the children sometimes being teenaged prostitutes. This can add up to hundreds of youngsters over a period of several years. Most pedophiles are physically nonviolent.

Why Castration Works

Let's also be clear about castration. Many people believe that castrating a sex offender is like cutting off the hand of the crook. Not so. Cutting off the penis would be like cutting off the hand of the crook, but that is not what castration is. Surgical castration involves removal of the testes only. When the penis is removed but the testes are still left intact, a man will still try to have sex. If the testes are removed, but the penis left intact, a man is far less likely to attempt to engage in sexual behavior. Removal of the testes generally decreases the desire for sexual activity, rather than affecting the capacity to perform.

The testes are the major source of testosterone production in males. It is the marked elevation in testosterone in males at the time of puberty that is associated with a marked increase in sexual desire and interest. Lowering testosterone can reduce the intensity of sexual desire.

A man can will his right arm to move. He cannot will an erection. He can get an erection by thinking certain thoughts. Tragically, for him and for the rest of us, Mr. McQuay apparently discovered that thoughts and cravings about children are what arouse him. To be afflicted with such a condition can itself be a nightmare. It is a condition that cannot be willed, legislated, or punished away. Reported rates of recidivism in the scientific literature for pedophiles not receiving treatment have varied considerably. It's difficult to know whether a given pedophile has not re-offended or simply re-offended and not been caught. Recidivism rates could, however, be as high as 65 percent. This figure makes intuitive sense: If one goes to prison because of a sexual attraction to 10-year-old boys, there is nothing about being in prison that will erase that attraction.

> *"Lowering testosterone can reduce the intensity of sexual desire."*

The good news is that lowering testosterone levels works. One Danish study reported a 4.3 percent recidivism rate over a period of up to 18 years among 117 surgically castrated sex offenders, whereas 58 non-castrated offenders were 10 times more likely to re-offend. A 7.4 percent recidivism rate was reported among 121 castrated sex offenders in Switzerland over five years compared with a 52 percent rate at the 10 year followup among men not undergoing the procedure. Yet another Danish study involving over 900 castrated sex offenders followed for periods of as long as 30 years reported a mere 2.2 percent recidivism rate.

Chemical Castration

Surgical castration, however, is neither necessary nor foolproof. Its effects can be reversed by taking testosterone. A better idea is so-called chemical castration. This involves no surgery—it consists of injections that lower testosterone levels. Compliance with medications used to lower testosterone can readily be monitored because they can be given by means of periodic injections. This treatment recently made headlines. In Florida, a legislative attempt is being made to impose testosterone-lowering injections upon possibly unwilling repeat offenders.

There is precedent in this country for compelling persons to undergo medical procedures without choice. At one time, because of the danger of smallpox, everyone was required to be vaccinated so that they would not pose a danger to the community. Convicted felons lose certain rights (e.g., the right to bear arms). If it were clear that a community would definitely be safer with a sexual offender's testosterone lowered, then society would likely have a right to insist that he make himself safe.

> *"If one goes to prison because of a sexual attraction to 10-year-old boys, there is nothing about being in prison that will erase that attraction."*

Lowering testosterone is not a cure, a guarantee, or a panacea, but it might be far more palatable to a society in which many people are squeamish about mandating surgical castration. In conjunction with psychological counseling, most testosterone-lowering treatments are effective, especially when used to help individuals who want to change. In combination—chemical castration and counseling—we've seen encouragingly low rates of recidivism; one study found a 15 percent rate, a figure which is deceptively high because the study broadly defined re-offending to include non-sexual contact, like visits to schoolyards.

Today most people still consider sexual offenses, even the many that are nonviolent, to be more a question for the legal system than one in which science and medicine can play a useful role. But like it or not, it is a fact that over 90 percent of incarcerated sex offenders sooner or later will be free. If legislation and punishment alone cannot fully solve the problem, medicine and science need to be called into action. And if society can be made safer by such means, why not use them? Mr. McQuay, we should remember, will be among us again soon.

Civil Commitment Laws Are Dangerous

by Barbara Dority

About the author: *Barbara Dority is executive director of the Washington Coalition Against Censorship, and cochair of the Northwest Feminist Anti-Censorship Task Force.*

On June 23, 1997, the U.S. Supreme Court ruled in *Kansas v. Hendricks* that the state may brand sex offenders as "violent sexual predators" and commit them indefinitely after they have served their full prison sentences, based on speculation about what they might do in the future.

In a majority opinion written by Justice Clarence Thomas, the Court also declared that indefinite civil confinement is not punishment, that the new definitions stated above do not violate due process rights, and that a yearly review of a person's confinement need not be conducted by an impartial court but can be facilitated by a special committee set up by the state and accountable to no one.

The Sexually Violent Predator Act

The case began with Kansas' 1994 Sexually Violent Predator Act, in which the state legislature established procedures for the "civil commitment" of persons who, due to a "mental abnormality" or a "personality disorder," are likely to engage in future "predatory acts of sexual violence." Although Kansas already had a long-standing statute regulating involuntary commitment of the "mentally ill," the legislature decided it was too narrowly drawn. In the act's preamble, the legislature states:

> A small but extremely dangerous group of sexually violent predators exist[s] who do not have a mental disease or defect that renders them appropriate for involuntary treatment pursuant to the [general involuntary civil commitment statute]. . . . In contrast to persons appropriate for civil commitment, sexually violent predators generally have anti-social personality features which are unamenable to existing mental illness treatment modalities, and those features

Reprinted from Barbara Dority, "Shades of the Gulag," *The Humanist*, January/February 1998. Reprinted with permission from the author.

render them likely to engage in sexually violent behavior. The legislature further finds that sexually violent predators' likelihood of engaging in repeat acts of predatory sexual violence is high. The legislature further finds that the prognosis for rehabilitating sexually violent predators in a prison setting is poor, the treatment needs of this population are very long term and treatment modalities are very different than traditional treatments.

To address this perceived problem, the legislature established a "civil commitment procedure for the long term care and treatment of the sexually violent predator" and defines a sexually violent predator as

any person who has been convicted of or charged with a sexually violent offense and who suffers from a mental abnormality or personality disorder which makes the person likely to engage in predatory acts of sexual violence.

The act requires the custodial agency to notify the local prosecutor sixty days before the anticipated release of a person who might meet the act's criteria. Within forty-five days, the prosecutor must decide whether to petition the state for the person's involuntary commitment. After a professional evaluation, a trial is held to determine beyond a reasonable doubt whether the individual can be classified under the new standards as a sexually violent predator.

Kansas filed a petition to commit Leroy Hendricks, who had a history of sexually molesting children and was scheduled for release from prison. The court reserved ruling on Hendricks' challenge to the act's constitutionality but granted his request for a jury trial, in which it was determined that he was a sexually violent predator. Finding that pedophilia qualifies as a "mental abnormality" under the act, the court ordered him committed.

> *"[Civil commitment] amounts to little more than disguised punishment."*

On appeal, the Kansas Supreme Court invalidated the act on the grounds that the precommitment condition of a "mental abnormality" did not satisfy the "substantive" due process requirement that involuntary civil commitment must be predicated on a "mental illness" finding.

The Supreme Court Upholds Civil Commitment

On June 23, 1997, the U.S. Supreme Court reversed the state court's ruling on appeal, upholding the act. The High Court found that the law "presented no constitutional violations"—that it does not violate the Constitution's double jeopardy prohibition or its ban on ex post facto lawmaking. In the past, the Court has only upheld involuntary civil commitment statutes that detain people who are unable to control their behavior and pose a danger to the public health and safety, provided the confinement takes place pursuant to proper procedures and evidentiary standards.

The U.S. Supreme Court also rejected the claim that the act is necessarily punitive because it fails to offer any legitimate treatment. Yet, without treatment, confinement under the act amounts to little more than disguised punishment. (According to the testimony of Terry Davis, Kansas' director of quality assurance, confinement takes place in the psychiatric wing of a prison hospital where those confined by the act and ordinary prisoners are treated alike.)

In addition, the Court said that a prisoner can be forced to testify at the commitment trial and that all past charges—whether or not proven—may be entered into evidence. In fact, it granted the states powers for which Kansas did not ask. The justices said the law could also be used against persons never convicted of a crime.

It is a well-established precedent that the state's power of civil commitment may only be invoked under extremely narrow circumstances: in cases where people have obvious, severe mental conditions—like schizophrenia or psychosis—that break their link with reality or make them an immediate danger to themselves or others. In short, the state's power to lock up people has been acceptable only because of its limited, clear scope.

Psychiatry concerns itself with a vast gray area of mental traits and conditions, ranging from nicotine addiction to sadomasochism to "borderline personality disorders," that do not affect basic rationality or reality comprehension. These, and many others, have never been considered mental illnesses or grounds for involuntary commitment.

Indefinite Punishment

The High Court, in fact, explicitly endorsed this distinction in 1992 by ruling that states may not involuntarily commit people who are dangerous unless they are also mentally ill. With any threshold for commitment lower than mental illness—such as "personality disorder"—practically any prisoner can be indefinitely locked into a psychiatric ward. Interestingly, the Court stated in this ruling that most people in prison have a "personality disorder" and that every prisoner, by virtue of having committed crimes, could be seen as predisposed to do so again. Any standard that broad, the Court said, has to be wrong.

Clearly, since the act does not provide any treatment until after a prisoner's release date, how can it be anything but an effort to inflict further punishment? In any event, the ex post facto clause should prohibit the act's application to those whose crimes were committed prior to its enactment.

These offenders were not determined to have a mental abnormality

"[Civil commitment] is an attempt to extend prison sentences."

when they were originally sentenced, nor do these laws contain any guidelines or treatment goals. "This is not an attempt to gain treatment or anything close to that," says Howard Zonana, professor of psychiatry at Yale University and a spokesperson for the American Psychiatric Association. "What this really is is an attempt to extend prison sentences."

The Kansas Supreme Court correctly found that, as of the time of Hendricks' commitment, the state had not funded treatment or entered into treatment contracts and had little, if any, qualified treatment staff. According to the commitment program's own director, Hendricks received "essentially no treatment" during the first ten months beyond his prison sentence that he has already been detained. Since the act explicitly defers diagnosis, evaluation, and commitment proceedings until a few weeks prior to release, we must ask why the state wouldn't commit and require treatment of sex offenders sooner, say right after they begin to serve their sentences?

> *"[Civil commitment] laws undermine our fundamental conception of liberty by advancing the practice of preventive detention."*

An act that simply seeks confinement wouldn't need to begin civil commitment proceedings sooner, would it? Proceedings would begin only when an offender's prison term ends, providing treatment years after the criminal act that indicated its necessity. Experts say delaying treatment leads to loss of memory and makes it more difficult for the offender to accept responsibility; time in prison leads to attitude hardening that one expert says "engender[s] a distorted view of the precipitating offense." Obviously, if long-term treatment (rather than further punishment) were Kansas' primary aim, the state would require that treatment begin soon after conviction, not ten or more years later.

As it happens, in a previous ruling, the High Court has said that a failure to consider or to use "alternative and less harsh methods" to achieve a nonpunitive objective can help to show that the legislature's purpose "was to punish." In fact, we find "least restrictive alternativ[e]" provisions in the ordinary civil commitment laws of almost all states. But these statutes do not require the committing authority to consider the possibility of using less restrictive alternatives, such as post-release supervision, halfway houses, and the like.

A Misuse of Psychiatry

The Washington State Psychiatric Association (WSPA) filed an amicus brief in the Hendricks case, strongly opposing the law as a misuse of psychiatry. (Washington State as a similar law.) Since the term mental abnormality has no clinical meaning or recognized diagnostic use, mental illness is not synonymous with mental disorder.

The WSPA brief states: "Many, perhaps most, of the mental disorders described in the *Diagnostic and Statistical Manual (4th Ed.)* would certainly not be regarded as a 'mental illness' for purposes of involuntary commitment." It also cites examples—male erectile disorder, female orgasmic disorder, caffeine-induced sleep disorder, nightmare disorder, and nicotine use disorder—before continuing:

Any argument that "mental illness" and "mental disorder" are synonymous flies in the face of common sense and sound psychiatric practice. To be identified as "mentally ill," a person must be suffering from a serious cognitive, perceptual, or affective dysfunction which significantly impairs their ability to function in ordinary life. In the absence of such an impairment, a diagnosis of "mental illness" would never be warranted. . . . Certainly some sex offenders suffer from a mental disorder, and some are undoubtedly "mentally ill." However, the fact of being a sex offender does not, in itself, imply a mental disorder or mental illness. Deviant behavior which is criminal does not in itself constitute a mental disorder.

In conclusion, the WSPA states:

These laws undermine our fundamental conception of liberty by advancing the practice of preventive detention. Violent sex offenders who represent a long-term threat to public safety should receive sentences commensurate with their crimes. It does not facilitate a sound and responsible use of psychiatric knowledge to incarcerate them under the guise of "commitment." Offenders who are truly mentally ill can and should be committed under Kansas' preexisting involuntary treatment act. It is precisely because sex offenders are typically not mentally ill that the Kansas legislature took the remarkable and unfortunate step that it did.

The Group for the Advancement of Psychiatry, the President's Commission on Mental Health, and the American Bar Association have also urged that these laws be repealed.

A Dangerous Law

Other states are now rushing to pass statutes modeled after the Kansas law and to expand existing ones. The number of men (as yet there are no women) committed under these laws is already in the hundreds. Zonana says that, as more states adopt these laws, about 10 percent of the people now in prison on "sex charges" could end up committed, leading to tens of thousands within a few years.

America's current obsession with crime has helped to swell our prison population to over 1.7 million—more than any democracy in the history of the world. For anyone snared in America's sex laws—which, remember, include everything from statutes criminalizing public sex, indecent exposure, sodomy, lewd and lascivious conduct, and violation of age-of-consent laws—the threat of indefinite imprisonment now looms large.

The most chilling aspect of the U.S. Supreme Court's decision is that it established the right of lawmakers to draft laws permitting the involuntary commitment of any "narrowly defined class" of citizens they decide presents a "future dangerousness" to the state and suffers from whatever "mental abnormality" they designate. How much of a leap is it to classify "persistent drug abusers" as suffering from a "mental abnormality" that predisposes them to commit "future acts of dangerousness"? How much will it take to declare that various types of political dissidents suffer from a "personality disorder" that predisposes them to commit future acts of civil disobedience?

This Court ruling overturns what has always been a tenet of American jurisprudence: that people are punished for crimes the state has proven were committed, not crimes the state contends they might commit in the future.

Castration Will Not Prevent Child Molestation

by Gina Kolata

About the author: *Gina Kolata is an author and a reporter for the* New York Times.

The California solution for child molesters sounds so simple—just castrate them, or make them take a chemical that takes away their sex drive, and they will offend no more. The plan comes at a time when both political parties are vying to see who can be toughest on crime. And it targets the criminals Americans find most disgusting.

But as the California legislature sends its bill on child molesters to the Governor [Pete Wilson signed the law and it went into effect in January 1997], mental health experts who treat sex offenders and legal experts who deal with them say that, alas, it's not so simple. Leaving aside the question of whether this legislation can overcome constitutional challenges, experts say that virtually everything being assumed about child molesters and about castration, chemical or surgical, is a myth, a leap of faith, or just plain wrong.

Exaggerated Statistics

The bill's supporters, for example, assume that child molesters are more likely than other criminals to repeat the crime. Assemblyman Bill Hoge of Pasadena, California, the chief sponsor of the bill, said that child molesters, when released from prison, "will repeat this crime again at least 90 percent of the time." His bill would require any pedophile convicted of a second offense to undergo surgical castration or to take a drug that reduces testosterone levels to pre-pubertal levels. The same fate would befall a man whose first crime was sufficiently terrible.

A 90 percent recidivism rate? That is a gross exaggeration, legal and medical experts say.

It is "a folk belief," said Frank Zimring, a law professor at the University of California at Berkeley. "The recidivism rates of child molesters are lower than

Reprinted from Gina Kolata, "The Many Myths About Sex Offenders," *The New York Times*, September 1, 1996. Reprinted with permission from *The New York Times*.

in other crimes," he said. "They are in the teens or twenties, depending on how long you follow up."

In contrast, said Dr. Marvin Wolfgang, a sociologist at the University of Pennsylvania, a large study conducted by the Department of Justice found that 46 percent of all felons were convicted of a felony again within three years after they were released from prison.

Although the percentage of American men who are child molesters is unknown, in Canada, said Dr. Ronald Langevin, a psychiatrist at the University of Toronto, they make up about 1/20th of 1 percent of the population.

But even so, why not stop them from their heinous crimes? "Why not give these people a shot to calm them down and bring them under control or, alternatively, give them the option of going under the knife?" Mr. Hoge asked.

No Evidence

The problem, some say, is that there is no good evidence that drugs, or even castration, prevent child molestation. Both methods have been tried on a voluntary basis but neither has been put to a scientific test and no country has made these treatments mandatory. As it stands now, it is difficult to tell if men who received treatment subsequently commit fewer crimes because of the treatment itself or because they were motivated enough to ask for it.

Of course, most men do not want the treatment, said Dr. Langevin. He attempted a study at the Clark Institute of Psychiatry in Toronto, asking 100 child molesters if they would agree to be randomly assigned to take anti-testosterone pills or placebos. "Only 18 agreed to take the pills for three months," he said, and after three months only 12 remained in the study, one of whom confessed that he had been flushing his pills down the toilet.

The Problems with Castration

Dr. Langevin said the medications can reduce thoughts of sex, at least temporarily, but men can still have erections. He added that not everyone responds to the drugs and that some who initially respond eventually become inured. The drugs can make men grow breasts and can make them gain weight. In the long term, said Dr. William Bremner, an endocrinologist at the University of Washington in Seattle, the drugs can make men more like old women, causing them to lose bone and muscle and to suffer premature osteoporosis.

> *"Experts say that virtually everything being assumed about child molesters and about castration . . . is a myth, a leap of faith, or just plain wrong."*

Which raises another problem with anti-testosterone drugs. They can be counteracted with shots of steroids like the ones used by some body builders. "It wouldn't take a rocket scientist to get androgens to crank up their sexual functioning," Dr. Bremner said.

Another complication, said Dr. Raymond Rosen, professor of psychiatry at the Robert Wood Johnson Medical School in New Brunswick, New Jersey, is that only about 60 percent of men who have sex with children are motivated by uncontrollable sexual urges. Others, he said, are "acting out aggressively with women or children," while others "are criminal types who will break society's laws in any way they can." He added that there is no evidence that drugs or castration will be effective against the antisocial or aggressive criminals and, in fact, he said, most studies of the drug "did all they could to screen these people out."

> *"There is no good evidence that drugs, or even castration, prevent child molestation."*

The Alcoholic Connection

Dr. Langevin said that most sex offenders are alcoholics—as many as 76 percent of sex offenders sent to a Toronto penitentiary over a three-year period abused alcohol, he found, and about half committed their crimes when drunk. Maybe the California legislature should require antabuse, the anti-alcohol drug, he said, only half-facetiously, adding that it also reduces sexual urges.

The lack of good data on the effects of castration or drugs on recidivism among sex criminals, and the fact that no one has ever done a scientific study to show these treatments help solve the problem, makes the California bill alarming, Mr. Zimring said.

"What you are looking at is the dynamics of ignorance in action," he said. "This is 'don't bother me with the facts' legislation."

Decades ago, Mr. Zimring said, when social scientists started dabbling with eugenics, sterilizing criminals and the insane, "the horror was what we would do in the name of science." But, he said, as terrible as that was, he considers the current movement worse. "This is a celebration of not needing any scientific information or controls on punishment policy," he said. "And that naked aggression is much scarier."

Bibliography

Books

Elizabeth Bartholet	*Nobody's Children: Abuse and Neglect, Foster Drift, and the Adoption Alternative.* Boston: Beacon Press, 2000.
John Briere, Lucy Berliner, and Josephine A. Bulkley, eds.	*The APSAC Handbook on Child Maltreatment.* Newbury Park, CA: Sage, 2000.
Byrgen Finkelman	*Child Abuse: A Multidisciplinary Survey: Physical and Emotional Abuse and Neglect.* New York: Garland, 1995.
Richard B. Gartner	*Betrayed as Boys: Psychodynamic Treatment of Sexually Abused Men.* New York: Guilford Press, 1999.
Mary Edna Helfer, Ruth S. Kempe, and Richard D. Krugman, eds.	*The Battered Child.* Chicago: University of Chicago Press, 1999.
Sandra K. Hewitt	*Assessing Allegations of Sexual Abuse in Preschool Children: Understanding Small Voices.* Newbury Park, CA: Sage, 2000.
Philip Jenkins	*Pedophiles and Priests: Anatomy of a Contemporary Crisis.* New York: Oxford University Press, 1996.
Richard Kagan	*Turmoil to Turning Points: Building Hope for Children in Crisis Placements.* New York: W.W. Norton, 1996.
Karen L. Kinnear	*Childhood Sexual Abuse: A Reference Handbook.* Santa Barbara, CA: ABC-CLIO, 1995.
Anna J. Michener	*Becoming Anna: The Autobiography of a Sixteen-Year-Old.* Chicago: University of Chicago Press, 1998.
Ronald T. Potter-Efron and Patricia S. Potter-Efron, eds.	*Aggression, Family Violence, and Chemical Dependency.* Binghamton, NY: Haworth, 1996.
Andren Schoen and Brian Prats	*Beyond the Big Easy: One Man's Triumph Over Abuse.* Tempe, AZ: New Falcon, 2000.
Sue William Silverman	*Because I Remember Terror, Father, I Remember You.* Athens: University of Georgia Press, 1999.

| Jane Waldfogel | *The Future of Child Protection: How to Break the Cycle of Abuse and Neglect.* Cambridge, MA: Harvard University Press, 1998. |

Periodicals

Arthur Allen	"She Catches Child Abusers," *Redbook,* March 1999.
Shawn Assael	"Child Abuse: Guilty Until Proven Innocent?" *Parents,* July 1995.
Matt Bai	"A Report from the Front in the War on Predators," *Newsweek,* May 19, 1997.
Nina Bernstein	"Old Pattern Cited in Missed Signs of Child Abuse," *New York Times,* July 22, 1999.
David Van Biema	"A Cheap Shot at Pedophilia? California Mandates Chemical Castration for Repeat Child Molesters," *Time,* September 9, 1996.
Rosemary Chalk and Patricia King	"Facing Up to Family Violence," *Issues in Science and Technology,* Winter 1998/1999.
James Collins	"Throwing Away the Key," *Time,* July 7, 1997.
Jennifer Couzin	"Missing the Signals: Doctors Misdiagnose Child-Abuse Injuries," *U.S. News & World Report,* March 1, 1999.
Skip Hollandsworth	"No One Knows What Could Be Happening to Those Kids," *Texas Monthly,* April 1999.
David Laskin	"Childproofing the Internet," *Parents,* January 1999.
Alex Morales	"Seeking a Cure for Child Abuse," *USA Today,* September 1998.
William Nack and Don Yaeger	"Every Parent's Nightmare," *Sports Illustrated,* September 13, 1999.
Marjorie Preston	"The Molester Next Door," *Ladies Home Journal,* July 1998.
Carla Rivera	"U.S. Child Abuse at Crisis Levels, Panel Says," *Los Angeles Times,* April 26, 1995.
Chris Nuttall Smith	"The Quiet Man," *New York,* July 19, 1999.
Rachel L. Swarns	"In a Policy Shift, More Parents Are Arrested for Child Neglect," *New York Times,* October 25, 1997.
Craig Daniel Turk	"Kinder Cut," *New Republic,* August 25, 1997.
Andrew Vachss	"Sex Predators Can't Be Saved," *New York Times,* January 5, 1995.
Gayle White	"Pain Relief," *Christianity Today,* July 12, 1999.
Daniel B. Wood	"Why Child Abuse Is at 10-Year Low: Recent Improvement Is Linked to the Strong Economy and Programs Targeting Prevention," *Christian Science Monitor,* May 1, 2000.
Howard Zonana	"The Civil Commitment of Sex Offenders," *Science,* November 14, 1997.

Organizations to Contact

The editors have compiled the following list of organizations concerned with the issues presented in this book. The descriptions are derived from materials provided by the organizations. All have publications or information available for interested readers. The list was compiled on the date of publication of the present volume; the information provided here may change. Be aware that many organizations take several weeks or longer to respond to inquiries, so allow as much time as possible.

ACT for Kids
7 S. Howard, Suite 200, Spokane, WA 99201-3816
(509) 747-8224 • fax: (509) 747-0609
e-mail: info@actforkids.org • website: www.actforkids.org

ACT for Kids is a nonprofit organization that provides resources, consultation, research, and training for the prevention and treatment of child abuse and sexual violence. The organization's publications include workbooks, manuals, and the books *My Very Own Book About Me* and *How to Survive the Sexual Abuse of Your Child.*

American Academy of Child and Adolescent Psychiatry (AACAP)
3615 Wisconsin Ave. NW, Washington, DC 20016-3007
(202) 966-7300 • fax: (202) 966-2891
website: www.aacap.org

AACAP supports and advances child and adolescent psychiatry through research and the distribution of information. The academy's goal is to provide information that will ensure proper treatment for children who suffer from mental or behavioral disorders due to child abuse, molestation, or other factors. AACAP publishes fact sheets on a variety of issues concerning disorders that may affect children and adolescents.

American Professional Society on the Abuse of Children (APSAC)
407 S. Dearborn, Suite 1300, Chicago, IL 60605
(312) 554-0166 • fax: (312) 554-0919
e-mail: APSACMems@aol.com • website: www.apsac.org

APSAC is dedicated to improving the coordination of services in the fields of child abuse prevention, treatment, and research. It publishes a quarterly newsletter, the *Advisor,* and the *Journal of Interpersonal Violence.*

False Memory Syndrome Foundation
3401 Market St., Suite 130, Philadelphia, PA 19104-3315
(215) 387-1865 • (800) 568-8882 • fax: (215) 387-1917
website: www.fmsonline.org

The foundation believes that many "delayed memories" of sexual abuse are the result of false memory syndrome (FMS). In FMS, patients in therapy "recall" childhood abuse that never occurred. The foundation seeks to discover reasons for the spread of FMS, works for the prevention of new cases, and aids FMS victims, including those falsely accused of abuse. The foundation publishes a newsletter and various papers and distributes articles and information on FMS.

National Center for Missing & Exploited Children (NCMEC)
699 Prince St., Alexandria, VA 22314-3175
(703) 274-3900• fax: (703) 274-2220
hot line: (800) THE-LOST (843-5678)
website: www.missingkids.org

NCMEC serves as a clearinghouse of information on missing and exploited children and coordinates child protection efforts with the private sector. A number of publications on these issues are available, including guidelines for parents whose children are testifying in court, help for abused children, and booklets such as *Children Traumatized in Sex Rings* and *Child Molesters: A Behavioral Analysis.*

National Clearinghouse on Child Abuse and Neglect Information
330 C St. SW, Washington, DC 20447
(703) 385-7565 • (800) 394-3366 • fax: (703) 385-3206
e-mail: nccanch@calib.com • website: www.calib.com/nccanch

This national clearinghouse collects, catalogs, and disseminates information on all aspects of child maltreatment, including identification, prevention, treatment, public awareness, training, and education. The clearinghouse offers various reports, fact sheets, and bulletins concerning child abuse and neglect.

National Coalition Against Domestic Violence (NCADV)
Child Advocacy Task Force
PO Box 18749, Denver, CO 80218-0749
(303) 839-1852 • fax: (303) 831-9251
website: www.ncadv.org

NCADV represents organizations and individuals that assist battered women and their children. The Child Advocacy Task Force deals with issues affecting children who witness violence at home or are themselves abused. It publishes the *Bulletin,* a quarterly newsletter.

National Criminal Justice Reference Service (NCJRS)
U.S. Department of Justice
PO Box 6000, Rockville, MD 20849-6000
(301) 519-5500 • (800) 851-3420
e-mail: askncjrs@ncjrs.org • website: www.ncjrs.org

A research and development agency of the U.S. Department of Justice, NCJRS was established to prevent and reduce crime and to improve the criminal justice system. Among its publications are *Resource Guidelines: Improving Court Practice in Child Abuse and Neglect Cases* and *Recognizing When a Child's Injury or Illness Is Caused by Abuse.*

Prevent Child Abuse America (PCAA)
200 S. Michigan Ave., 17th Fl., Chicago, IL 60604-2404
(312) 663-3520• fax: (312) 939-8962
e-mail: mailbox@preventchildabuse.org • website: www.preventchildabuse.org

PCAA's mission is to prevent all forms of child abuse. It distributes and publishes materials on a variety of topics, including child abuse and child abuse prevention. *Talking About Child Sexual Abuse* and *Basic Facts About Child Sexual Abuse* are among the various pamphlets PCAA offers.

The Safer Society Foundation
PO Box 340, Brandon, VT 05733-0340
(802) 247-3132 • fax: (802) 247-4233
e-mail: ray@usa-ads.net • website: www.safersociety.org

The Safer Society Foundation is a national research, advocacy, and referral center for the prevention of sexual abuse of children and adults. The Safer Society Press publishes research, studies, and books on treatment for sexual victims and offenders and on the prevention of sexual abuse.

Survivor Connections
52 Lyndon Rd., Cranston, RI 02905-1121
(401) 941-2548 • fax: (401) 941-2335
e-mail: scsitereturn@hotmail.com • website: www.angelfire.com/ri/survivorconnections/

Survivor Connections is an activist center for survivors of incest, rape, sexual assault, and child molestation. It publishes the newsletter *Survivor Activist*

United Fathers of America (UFA)
6360 Van Nuys Blvd., Suite 8, Van Nuys, CA 91401
(818) 785-1440 • fax: (818) 995-0743
e-mail: info@unitedfathers.com
websites: www.fathersunited.com • www.fathersforever.com (a branch of UFA)

UFA helps fathers fight for the right to remain actively involved in their children's upbringing after divorce or separation. UFA believes that children should not be subject to the emotional and psychological trauma caused when vindictive parents falsely charge ex-spouses with sexually abusing their children. Primarily a support group, UFA answers specific questions and suggests articles and studies that illustrate its position.

VOCAL/National Association of State VOCAL Organizations (NASVO)
7485 E. Kenyon Ave., Denver, CO 80237
hot line: (303) 233-5321
e-mail: vocal@vocal.org • website: www.nasvo.org

VOCAL (Victims of Child Abuse Laws) provides information, research data, referrals, and emotional support for those who have been falsely accused of child abuse. NASVO maintains a library of research on child abuse and neglect issues, focusing on legal, mental health, social, and medical issues, and will provide photocopies of articles for a fee. It publishes the bimonthly newsletter *NASVO News.*

Index